QUANTUM PA

A 21st Century Analysis of the Paranormal Phenomena

PATRICK JACKSON

GHOST

/gōst/ /goʊst

NOUN

1. An apparition of a dead person which is believed to appear or become manifest to the living,

Typically as a nebulous image.

'The building is haunted by the ghost of a monk; it is said that his ghost still haunts the crypt'

Synonyms:

spectre, phantom, wraith, spirit, soul, shadow, presence, vision, apparition, hallucination, bodach, Doppelgänger; duppy, informalspook, literaryphantasm, shade, revenant, visitant, wight; rare-eidolon, manes, lemures

In reality:

"Any sufficiently advanced technology Is indistinguishable from magic."

ARTHUR C. CLARKE

Introducing a new
PERSPECTIVE
on the paranormal phenomena
Answering more questions
Than the last two-hundred years of research.

WRITTEN BY PATRICK JACKSON

The following information is the result of twenty years experience of
paranormal observations, slowly building a logical model of what's
really going on. All performed on a next to zero budget, the
information presented shatters mainstream perceptions and
formulates a totally different perspective on the greatest mystery of
modern times...

Only those who attempt the absurd
Can achieve the impossible...

Albert Einstein

CONTENTS

How this book is presented:

The following text fairly and logically questions many core areas of paranormal experiences and activities.

The paranormal has a set belief system; within that system are common premeditated conclusions on observed paranormal actions and behaviours. These conclusions originated from 16th century analyses and have been passed on unquestioned for centuries.

Please note:

This book does not debunk the paranormal phenomena, but rather is an authentic and modern attempt to cut away the fog and see what is really going on.

INTRODUCTION:
THE BLACK SHEEP

My name is Patrick Jackson.

I grew up in a quiet little village just outside of Cambridge in England, a very quaint and down-to-earth part of the country. An area where the crime rate was almost zero— people left their doors open and drunk tea like it was going out of fashion.

It was so quiet that I would often say that I could have a nap in the middle of the road and wake up alive.

But this little place had a secret... my hometown was a hot bed of paranormal activity... so much so...

It became normal.

When you are born surrounded by something, you just don't realise how unusual this stuff is to the outside world.

One of the first paranormal experiences I witnessed was over at a friend's house. I was only eight or nine years-old and we were playing in the garden as we always did, messing around on his climbing frame and shooting at each other with cap guns.

We had a den, a small open area nestled within a dense tree line. It was about 30 feet deep and surrounded by trees and bushes –a wall of thorns and mud– you just couldn't get in from the other side.

I remember clearly; it was a summer afternoon during the weekend and we were on the climbing frame after running around playing hide-and-seek. Suddenly, a tall white figure walked out from the den opening.

It was completely pure white, and from the side its feet looked triangular. As it stood there looking ahead, I shouted, "Oi - get out of our den!" It turned, startled, and looked right at me; it had no face, just pure white. As it saw me, the tall figure turned around and quickly ducked back inside the den.

We both leapt off the frame and ran as fast as we could towards the opening, literally a couple of seconds behind it. But when we ducked in, no one was there. No tracks, no damage to the perimeter - nothing. My friend was confused, but I knew what I had seen.

At the time, I didn't relate it to anything paranormal. I didn't yet know anything about this phenomena; I was young and thought, "Well, that was just strange."

That was the start of many experiences over my time there.

A few years later, I was year 3 or 4 at Milton primary school, just up the road from my house. Again, it was a hot summer day, during lunchtime 12:30 to 1:30. It was around 1:15pm when I looked up across the field; I saw this small, spinning, silver, pyramid-like object in the sky. As I watched it, I noticed it wobbled a little from side to side. The object was low, I would say less than 300 feet up. It was just sitting in the sky seeming to be observing us all. Suddenly the bell went off signalling that lunch time had ended. With that, we went back inside and once again I didn't think much of it… it was just strange.

The only real place in the village for socializing was a little club (bar) now called The Old Forge. I used to head down there most Fridays or Saturdays. The community was so small you generally would see someone you knew in there.

The bar itself was just five minutes from my home and located next to a large playing field with a children's play area and one evening while waiting for the place to open, I was sitting on the swing minding my own business. I looked over across the playing field and saw a guy standing about thirty feet away dressed as a monk.

Yeah that's right... a full-on monk with his hood up! I just looked and thought it was some local crazy person that was having a joke. I just shouted at him, "You alright?" and this guy just stood there motionless.

This picked up my attention. I had a red laser pointer in my pocket—I shot it at him. I remember seeing the laser dot reflecting on the ground, then his legs, then up on his chest, and finally I got him right in the face.

To my surprise, he didn't twitch or react to the laser—there was no movement at all. And most interesting of all, I still couldn't see a face. It was just a black mass; the laser dot reflected off of it, but it was like hitting a black wall. After 10 - 15 seconds of doing this, I still had no reaction from him. I thought that was really strange, so I stood up and started walking towards him.

When I get to this point in the story, people ask me if I felt scared. The answer is no; this is my hometown, where I was raised, and the ground I stood on was like a part of me. It felt like this guy was intruding in my back garden, so I squared off at him.

As I got closer, I could see all the details on his outfit down to the creases in the clothing. It seriously looked like someone had just dumped a grey statue in the middle of the field and that's how I perceived it.

I continued walking, getting within a few meters and—it suddenly dissipated into thin air. It did rattle me a little bit, but I didn't equate it to a ghost-sighting at this stage. At the time, I still didn't know anything about the paranormal subject, so I just took what I saw as face value.

A few days later I was at The Old Forge again. I told a few of the old local's guys that I thought I had seen a monk across the field. Straight away one of them said, "Yep, that's the mad monk of Landbeach. He was hung here years ago for getting a local girl pregnant."

I was really surprised by this and needed a drink to process it...

This all occurred when I was approximately 20 / 23 years old over the years preceding this, I saw between 12 to 16 UFOs (unidentified flying objects). I saw them during both daytime and night time and in the distance and up close—some so close I could throw a stone at them. They just slowly flew over silently and peacefully, like they were just patrolling. These were not huge flying disks, but small orbs around the size of a tennis ball, flying low, slow, and silently just above the street lights. I called them *pearls of light* as the light didn't flicker, they were constant. My parents had always told me to be polite, so my default was to always excitedly wave and shout hello. This was happening in the days before smart phones and digital cameras came about, however. It wasn't just myself seeing things as many locals also mentioned they saw strange lights low in the sky. One night a friend randomly managed to get a photo of a UFO hovering over the local church grounds, as seen below.

Figure#1 *All Saints' Church, Landbeach, Green End, Landbeach, Cambridge CB25 9FD - Current day time image*

Figure#2 same as above but at night

This image Figure#2 was taken at night using **infra-red (IR) film**. The object wasn't visible at the time and was only identified after the film was developed. This single object matches the configuration of those spotted by the Mexican Air Force on March 05, 2004; eleven flying objects flew alongside the planes during an air patrol of a drug smuggling operation. The eleven UFOs could only be seen through the military plane's dome mounted IR-system, and could not be seen with the naked eye. Neither the crew nor ground personnel could see the craft with radar. Sceptics have dismissed the event on March 05, 2004 as oil platform burn-off flares, but the Mexican authorities stated that the elevation of the lights were clocked at a higher altitude than their own aircrafts. This is a very significant event as it was the first time a government encounter had come forth publicly.

Notice the same reflection on its underside as if the object is surrounded with a bubble; these phenomena were also invisible to the human eye and only spotted by the forward-looking IR camera.

Figure#3

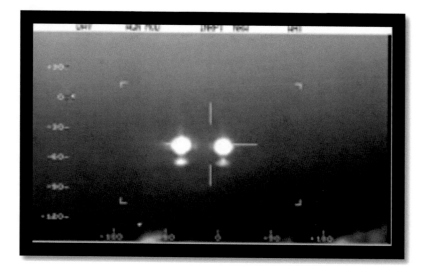

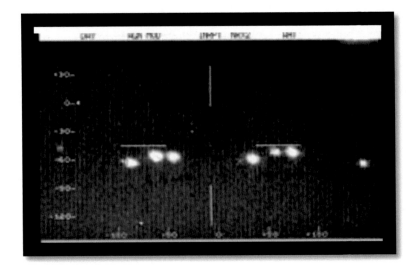

Reference: https://www.youtube.com/watch?v=Q2Rk9cpykwU

20 Years Later...

I now work in Information Technology (IT) as a Structured Query Language Database Administrator (SQL DBA) Specialist. My primary role is keeping dozens of high demand SQL servers running and secure. A big part of the job is a task called reverse engineering—or in other words, figuring stuff out fast when under pressure. When the databases stop working, the company stops making money, so you can imagine the stress. In every major company they have centralised databases that are the backbone of internal applications / functions and data analytics, this allows an application call B.I.Ds or Business Intelligence Development – that can provide near real-time data via pre-configured reports or real-time data via HTML web services. Part of the reverse engineering process is finding Correlations between datasets, noticing system behaviours and traits...

An example of this was when I was sent to fix a SQL system in a bank, the SQL server would just randomly crash out without warning or errors bring the bank itself to a halt. Even though I had no errors to work with it was possible to figure out what was going on. By watching the time pattern I noticed it started crashing from 10am in the morning, and nothing till 2pm (after lunch) I enquired who is running reports or scripts against the server at these times.

After ten minutes we identified who it could be and called them... After speaking I asked to rerun the same script – and as they did - the server crashed... Once I identified this they stopped the daily script run and the bank finally stabilised.

The problem was the script was returning a huge dataset (millions of lines) this data is then pushed to a buffer within the application, but the dataset was too large for the buffer – resulting in a lock - bringing the server down. This only had started recently as was due to an application upgrade where the buffer was unknowingly reduced in size.

Overall - Reverse engineering is the process used when one needs to figure out a complex issue; this can be done in a number of ways. In the world of IT, developers come and go. A developer will often create something that a firm grows to depend on, and **no one knows how it works;** You would have thought developers would document it all as part of the job, but generally no. They typically have a backlog of work pending, so they just push on with the next project.

This could be a process, or a bit of code, but *a system* of some sort. So, people like me have to reverse engineer it—create documentation explaining how it works to allow the system to be modified to current requirements, fixed, etc.

Over the years I have reversed engineered everything from processes to problems within accounting systems, document management systems, to corporate database systems. I should mention that reverse engineering is nothing amazing, as this is common practice within IT. Every day IT professionals are figuring out how stray processes or issues work and how they can be fixed. How we do this is simple—*it is not what you know, but how one's mind processes and connects information.* I was far from a genius at school, but some people can just cut through the noise and see structures, patterns, and relationships that create logic. From there, it is just connecting the dots and solving the puzzle.

Because of my unique experiences while I was growing-up, my evening TV obsession was (and still is) watching paranormal shows. I was trying to find clues on what was really going on, trying to find patterns and common actions that connect to logic of some kind. At the same time, I obsessively watched performers such as David Copperfield, and more recently, Dynamo, demonstrating illusions. My poor eyes have spent many nights bleeding from hours of replaying tricks; I just have to figure out how they do things.

I have never been one to believe in magic or miracles, but I do believe in **mechanisms**—mechanisms that can *appear* to be magic… even supernatural.

Mechanism

/ˈmɛk(ə)nɪz(ə)m/Submit
noun
1. *a system of parts working together in a machine; a piece of machinery.*

"a third motor powers the tape eject mechanism"

---

synonyms: apparatus, machine, appliance, tool, device, implement, utensil, instrument, contraption, contrivance, gadget, tackle, structure, system; More

2. *a natural or established process by which something takes place or is brought about.*

"the immune system's mechanism for detecting pathogens"

synonyms: procedure, process, system, operation, method, technique, workings, means, medium, agency, channel, channels, vehicle, structure

For example:

An illusionist performs a trick. To the watching crowd he just performed the impossible. In reality his or her performance is a very well-crafted mechanism with many small unnoticeable actions (a.k.a. processes) in a controlled environment. The processes come together in a perfectly timed fashion to create the perception of magic. In real-time, one will not observe these small actions; only when you watch frame-by-frame and analyse everything, including the camera angles, does the illusion start to unwind. Once you spot the first action, the rest just shines out.

The day came when I wondered if I could apply the same reverse engineering techniques from IT to understanding the paranormal— ghosts, to be specific. Figuring out what they could be/what they are doing/ maybe replicate or trigger them somehow? I really wondered *how deep down the rabbit hole I could go?* To my knowledge, this subject has never been approached in this way before.

When I mentioned I was interested in doing this, my co-workers hit a wall of disbelief. I found that they not only were not interested in the subject, but they totally denied it existed at all! More interestingly, they refused to come with me to check out haunted locations.

"*No help here*," I thought. Like anything—if you want something done—do it yourself.

I observed online paranormal groups and found that the fan base had been an echo chamber for years—no new ideas or theories of what is occurring or why. It seemed to be a locked pseudoscience where people just take on the traditional beliefs and fly with it unquestioned.

I started asking some polite, but tough, questions within the online communities, the reaction…well… was not friendly. In the end, I got banned from every group I joined within three days.

I realised that the paranormal isn't just an idea or perception,

But a much loved belief system considered equal to religion.

Hard questions are not welcomed or even tolerated.

"The very concept of objective truth is fading out of the world, but lies will pass into history…"

George Orwell

As a result of my persistent questioning, I became the outcast. I was banned by community groups, the online paranormal radio stations heard about me but turned the other cheek, and even well-known researchers refused to engage with me. The few times they did open themselves to debate—the traditional paranormal ideas they embraced were quickly broken down. I even went to the extreme of offering a financial reward for anyone who could beat me in a debate, hundreds of comments later the general paranormal community failed to beat the logic I was presenting.

It reached a point that even friends who ran YouTube channels thought I was too extreme and would only agree to work with me under certain conditions – these conditions were understandable as they didn't want to alienate other group's belief systems, it would appear that the paranormal community can be quite fickle – all in a race to become the next paranormal TV top dog and internal networking via social media is the medium of choice. My presence and study caused nothing but friction and upset, truthfully I have forgotten how many times I have been banned or blocked even screamed at for politely challenging the current ideas. My work didn't just rattle the paranormal community but also affected my own personal affairs with a highly religious (now ex) girlfriend deeply shaken by my thought process.

Once I was even asked to be in a paranormal documentary film, only to be cut out when my analysis of the subject was incompatible with the director's vision. I was that **annoying guy** that stood out, that everyone tried their best to avoid. In reality, I wasn't one to be extreme or rude, on the contrary I approached this subject the same way anyone would have approached a technical project at work.

Among friends I became known as… The Black Sheep

PART ONE

AN ANALYSIS OF TRADITIONAL AND WIDELY-ACCEPTED PARANORMAL THEORIES

The Argument for Stone Tape Theory

I would say just about everyone has gone into an old building and felt a change in atmosphere at some point. Some buildings feel **oppressive and suffocating,** and indeed many of these old buildings do have stories of ghost sightings.

The Stone Tape Theory is all about the same event repeating itself. For example, a lady coming down the same stairs wearing the same clothes, or a ghost of a man walking through an empty derelict jail or hospital. In effect like a video tape is getting played back time and time again – it is said these *spirits* are not interactive but like a replay of history

The paranormal community conclude that these are classed as **residual sightings**. These ghosts are said to be *not interactive*, acting more like a projection from the past.

If it is a projection, then *something* must be storing the projection information somewhere...

Reference: *https://www.forensic-architecture.org/lexicon/stone-tape-theory/*

- *"The Stone Tape Theory speculates that inanimate materials can absorb energy from living beings. In other words, a 'recording' or track is laid down during moments of high tension, such as murder. This stored energy can consequently be released, resulting in a display of the recorded activity. The replay can take the form of a full manifestation or partial sounds such as voices or footsteps. Paranormal investigators commonly refer to such phenomena as residual hauntings. Ghosts are not spirits but non-interactive recordings similar to the registration capacities of an audiotape machine that can playback previously recorded events. While the theory may explain some ghostly sightings, no one knows what the recorded energy actually is. However, the possibility that it could be composed by our natural electric and magnetic fields is one of the explanations that the Stone Tape Theory advances."*

On the face of it, it sounds generally reasonable... a "theory" that has many grey areas but *sounds* kind of believable.

Let's break it down.

Technical Analysis

Right from the start we have a lot of red flags. Every scientific theory starts as an idea **and only after enough evidence** accumulates to support a **hypothesis**, it moves to the next step of the scientific method known as a **theory**. Only after completing this step can it become accepted as a valid explanation of a phenomenon. Remember, a scientific theory is the framework for observations and facts.

Reference: *https://www.livescience.com/21491-what-is-a-scientific-theory-definition-of-theory.html*

- **A scientific hypothesis** is the suggested definition for an *unexplained occurrence* that doesn't fit into a currently accepted scientific theory.

- In other words, according to the Merriam-Webster Dictionary, a hypothesis is an idea that hasn't been proven yet.

Technically, this idea should really be called the Stone Tape Hypothesis.

The Stone tape idea was first introduced

Reference: *https://en.wikipedia.org/wiki/Stone_Tape*

In 1837 the polymath Charles Babbage published a work on natural theology called the Ninth Bridgewater Treatise. Babbage speculated that spoken words leave permanent impressions in the air, even though they become inaudible after time. He suggested that it is possible due to transfer of motion between particles.

The "Stone tape theory" could also be derived from the concept of "place memory". In the early days of the Society for Psychical Research place memory was considered an explanation for ghostly apparitions, seemingly connected with certain places. In the late 19th century, two of the SPR involved investigators, Edmund Gurney and Eleonor Sidgwick, presented views about certain buildings or materials being capable of storing records of past events,

This idea was then reinforced by the invention of **VHS and Betamax** tape.

Reference: *https://en.wikipedia.org/wiki/VHS*

*VHS (short for **Video Home System**) is a standard for consumer-level analog video recording on tape cassettes. Developed by Victor Company of Japan (JVC) in the early 1970s, it was released in Japan on September 9, 1976, and in the United States on August 23, 1977.*

Reference: *https://en.wikipedia.org/wiki/Betamax*

*Betamax (also called **Beta**, as in its logo) is a consumer-level analog-recording and cassette format of magnetic tape for video. It was developed by Sony and was released in Japan on May 10, 1975.*

Both of these tapes use a **magnetic imprinting** process to encode video and audio data on an **iron oxide coated Mylar tape**. This reinforced the stone tape idea to the paranormal mainstream, because certain bricks, stones and related building materials also contain iron oxide.

As a result, the existing research has generally concluded - that after death, as the spirit leaves the body, the spirit energy is imprinted into the walls and objects around them. Thus when objects that were dear to the deceased are moved, this creates activity, as the spirit energy that is attached to the object is disturbed.

One thing that became very apparent is the use of the word *spirit*. Spirit is not a bad word, but it's used as a blanket statement to fill in many gaps in understanding. For example, many people who stay in active areas for long periods state that activity *"follows them home"*.

When asked *"How does a ghost follow you home?"* Considering one may live hours away, had taken the London Underground, walked among hundreds of people though the city… *how* does it follow you home? The answer one gets from the paranormal community is, *"Well, because its spirit…"*

Defined as *"the non-physical part of a person which is the seat of emotions and character; the soul"*

In a nutshell, it is traditionally believed that iron oxide impregnated stone can **radiate electromagnetic fields** that can **induce feelings, project images, and even sounds** within the confines of a building.

I must admit, I can understand why the community came to this idea. During my research, I did notice that different buildings and areas had different feelings to them... Some would feel oppressive, while others feel very light, it's almost like feeling someone else's emotional baggage is bearing down on you, so what could be really going on?

"If you wish to understand the universe, think of energy, frequency and vibration."

Nikola Tesla

The reality is some building materials contain low levels of radioactive material; sandstone, concrete, brick, natural stone, gypsum, and granite all contain naturally occurring radioactive elements like radium, uranium, and thorium. Over time these naturally occurring elements can break down or decay into a radioactive gas called radon.

- Depending on the amount of the above materials present, may also cause small increases in ambient radiation levels. The level of this increase depends on the type and amounts of materials used.

What if these *different feelings* are in fact the natural response mechanism to constant low-level radioactive fields?

Fact: The human nervous system is bioelectrical.

- Bioelectricity

- Definition

Bioelectricity refers to electrical potentials and currents occurring within or produced by living organisms. It results from the conversion of chemical energy into electrical energy. Bioelectric potentials are generated by a number of different biological processes, and are used by cells to govern metabolism, to conduct impulses along nerve fibres, and to regulate muscular contraction. In most organisms, bioelectric potentials vary in strength from one to several hundred millivolts. The most important difference between bioelectric currents in living organisms and the type of electric current used to produce light, heat, or power is that a bioelectrical current is a flow of ions (atoms or molecules carrying an electric charge), while standard electricity is a movement of electrons.

Reference: *https://www.encyclopedia.com/medicine/encyclopedias-almanacs-transcripts-and-maps/bioelectricity*

Like all electrical systems, the human nervous system can be affected externally by some electronic fields or radiation.

Direct, bystander, and scatter low-dose radiation effects on the brain

- *To further explore the existence and mechanisms of low-dose radiation-induced direct and bystander changes, we analysed the effects of radiation on the brain, focusing on the hippocampus and the PFC due to their pivotal roles in memory, learning, and executive functions. We compared direct radiation and bystander radiation effects. Our recent study published in the Oncotarget (2016) was the first to conduct a large-scale analysis of the molecular, neuroanatomical, and behavioural consequences of direct and bystander low-dose irradiation on the rodent brain.41 The key findings were that: (i) direct head exposure to radiation doses as low as 24.5 cGy induced persistent, albeit small, increases in DNA damage, as measured by levels of γH2AX and effects on gene expression in the PFCs of exposed animals; (ii) bystander effects exist in the brain following liver irradiation and manifest as* **small increases in DNA damage,** *as measured by levels of γH2AX and alterations to gene and protein expressions; (iii) both head and liver irradiation reduce dendritic space (and, thus, synapse numbers) in measures of spine density, dendritic complexity, and dendritic length; (iv) the neuroanatomical effects are brain region-specific and are more pronounced in females; and (v) both head and liver irradiation alter behaviour.*

Reference:
https://www.ncbi.nlm.nih.gov/pmc/articles/PMC5531620/

Could it be possible that some people have a **higher sensitivity to low-dose radiation**? If so, could this not just have a small impact on DNA, but also a temporary electrical effect on the human nervous system? Could this effect result in a noticeable change in feelings as the nervous system translates this external interference?

At the moment the data is somewhat grey. Some scientists say external electronic fields/ low-level radiation from mobile phones or microwaves, for example, could be dangerous. Other scientists say low-dose radiation is totally safe, or at least within reason. Anecdotally, I personally work on computers all day and am constantly surrounded by electronic machines that continuously emit some level of electromagnetic field/ radiation. Interestingly, I have observed that I don't feel at all affected. If the electronic emissions from these mains powered computers and surrounding cables don't affect me, why would low level naturally occurring radiation from stone affect me?

One explanation - could be the different **frequencies** the electro-magnetic radiation is resonating at.

Reference: https://www.ncbi.nlm.nih.gov/books/NBK208983/

The effects of radiation on nervous tissues have been a subject of active investigation since changes in animal behaviour and nerve electrical properties were first reported in the Soviet Union during the 1950s and 1960s.1 RF radiation is reported to affect isolated nerve preparations, the central nervous system, brain chemistry and histology, and the blood-brain barrier.

The research is ongoing but it **could be the case** that different frequencies can create different responses in the body and mind. However, even if low-grade radiation could alter feelings & cause hallucinations, it would still not explain a number of key factors.

Altered feelings and hallucinations do not explain *multiple* people seeing *the same ghost at the same time* or even capturing that experience on camera.

So, what *is* causing this? Could it be stone recordings playing back at random?

The bottom line is, the process required to project 3D holographic moving images is complex and data intensive.

Reference:
https://www.researchgate.net/publication/254033574_3D_holograp
hic_display_and_its_data_transmission_requirement

- *During inline play-back of holographic video, hologram data are first read out from SSDs and buffered in main memory of loading PCs. There are 8 physical SSDs on 4 PCIe SSD cards in 2 loading PCs. Each physical SSD provides 281.1 MBps average sequential read speed. The total average read ability of hologram data is 2.25 GBps, which is sufficient for 9.44*

Gbps hologram data bandwidth requirement.

But, there is more. Not only does the Stone Tape Theory state that imprinted energy creates 3D visuals, the theory adds...

- *The replay can take the form of a full manifestation or partial sounds such as voices or footsteps.*

Audio replay is equally as complex as 3D imagery; the only way to create sound waves is through compression and expansion - shaping of air. A speaker system can replicate this mechanism to create sounds and music.

How do speakers work?

- *Speakers work by converting electrical energy into mechanical energy (motion). The mechanical energy compresses air and converts the motion into sound energy or sound pressure level (SPL).*
- *When an electric current is sent through a coil of wire, it induces a magnetic field.*
- *In speakers, a current is sent through the voice coil which produces an electric field that interacts with the magnetic field of the permanent magnet attached to the speaker.*
- *Like charges repel each other and different charges attract. As an audio signal is sent through the voice coil and the musical waveform moves up and down, the voice coil is attracted and repelled by the permanent magnet.*
- *This makes the cone that the voice coil is attached to move back and forth. The back and forth motion create pressure waves in the air that we perceive as sound.*

Reference: *https://blog.landr.com/how-do-speakers-work/*

In other words, to create moving 3D holograms and audio is a very complex technical process, requiring hundreds of thousands of subprocesses all working together perfectly, with high data transfer, processing, and dedicated hardware for the task.

The truth is stone **does not** have any observable chemical / atomic level capabilities to perform any of the above.

Example: Granite

*Granite is what is called a silica-rich rock. Though a complex process, pure silicon is extracted from granite by removing the oxygen, mixing it with carbon, and heating it within an electric arc furnace at 2,000+ degrees C. At those temperatures, the carbon reacts with the oxygen, becoming carbon dioxide and leaving pure silicon in the bottom of the furnace. This material can then be used as a semi-conductor—***perfect for central processing units a.k.a.*** silicon chips found in present-day computers and smart phones.*

Reference: https://mineralseducationcoalition.org/minerals-database/silica/

- *Silicon (Si) is a semi-metallic or metalloid, because it has several of the metallic characteristics. Silicon is never found in its natural state, but rather in combination with oxygen as the silicate ion SiO_4^{4-} in silica-rich rocks such as obsidian, granite, diorite, and sandstone. Feldspar and quartz are the most significant silicate minerals. Silicon alloys include a variety of metals, including iron, aluminium, copper, nickel, manganese and ferrochromium.*

The reality is, one could have a house built out of granite and that granite could be rich in silica. But that **doesn't mean** the house is a computer, or that it can process data of any kind. Regardless of how exotic the minerals that natural stone contains, without extraction/ filtering processes and clever engineering of that resource, it is next to useless in its natural state. Just because something contains the same chemical/mineral does not automatically allow it to have the same technical capabilities. Therefore one can logically make the argument that:

Iron oxide impregnated stone/rock is not responsible for paranormal activity (be that visual, physical/audible, or emotional).

However, later in the book I will mention a third element that could well be...

Time loops / Replaying of Past Events

The Argument for Time Slip Theory

Over the years there have been many stories of people observing spirits, many of which are wearing old clothing. Sometimes, entire scenes play out; even horse and carts have been witnessed kicking up dirt as they go by—only to vanish into thin air.

I dug around and found two such occurrences as documented by writer Nell Rose.

Reference: *https://exemplore.com/paranormal/The-Liverpool-Time-Slips-The-True-Story-Of-Mysterious-Occurences-In-Bold-Street*

The Story of Frank and Carol

In 1996, Frank and his wife, Carol, are out for a stroll in Liverpool town centre. Carol wanted to buy a book at Waterstone's, a large bookstore. As they approached Bold Street, Frank decided to go to another shop first; he bumped into a friend and stopped to chat in the street. Carol went ahead without him toward the bookstore. A few moments later, Frank said goodbye, visited the shop and turned to go back to meet his wife. After reaching Bold Street, he headed on towards the bookstore. As he approached, he glanced up and was surprised to see the name "Cripps" above the door. As he was about to cross over to see what was going on, a van swept past him with the name "Cardin's" on the side. The van drive honked his old-fashioned horn and drove past. Looking around, Frank suddenly realized that things were not quite what they should be. He looked at the cars driving past and realized that they were all old-fashioned vehicles from the 1950s and 60s. Then, he noticed the people. Men were wearing hats and macs (trench coats)s, and the women were dressed in full skirts with head scarves covering vintage pin curls. Frank was beginning to feel a bit freaked out.

He carried on crossing the road and headed towards the store. As he got closer, he noticed in the window there were handbags, shoes, and umbrellas. Suddenly, he saw a young woman looking up at the shop sign. She looked confused.

She was wearing modern clothes and as she saw him approaching, she smiled at him. Frank went into the shop, closely followed by the young woman. When they entered, he was surprised and pleased to see that it had indeed turned back into a bookshop. The young women smiled, shook her head and said, "That was strange, I thought it was a new clothes shop!" She walked away looking extremely puzzled.

This may sound an unlikely tale, however. Frank was a former police officer, who was used to dealing in facts, and definitely wasn't the type of person who would believe in the paranormal. Evidently, "Cripps" was indeed a women's shop that sold clothes and other goods decades before! Was this a time slip? Frank, for one, never stopped talking about it.

A Thief Goes Back to 1967

A young man named Sean, who, while shop lifting in Liverpool back in 2006, ran away from a Security Guard and headed down Hanover Street. Trying to shake off the Guard, Sean, 19, turned into a dead end street called Brookes Alley.

By this time he was out of breath and started to get a tight sensation in his chest. He soon realized that actually it wasn't a problem with him, but the atmosphere around him.

He waited for the Guard to come around the corner after him, but he never appeared. So, thinking he had given him the slip, he sauntered back out and started to walk down Hanover street again. But he soon realised that something was wrong.

The road looked different, and so did the pavement. He noticed cars driving by that looked very old fashioned, and the road works that he knew were there, were now gone.

Soon he saw that the people around him were wearing strange clothes. Crossing over to Bold Street, he noticed that there were traffic lights where they weren't before, and bushes growing around the Lyceum, near a bar that he recognized.

He carried on walking. Soon he began to feel that something was not quite right. Then he began to panic. He realized that somehow he had stepped back in Time. And the time slip was not going away.

Then he remembers his Cell phone. Taking it out of his pocket, he tried to get a signal, but of course it didn't work. Eventually he began to really panic, but soon spotted a kiosk selling newspapers and headed over.

Leaning over the Stand, he took a look at the front page of the Daily Post. There in bold lettering was the date. 18th May 1967.

He wondered what to do. What happens if he can't get back to his own time? What about family and friends?

So, speeding up his pace, he reached H. Samuel the Jewelers, and tried his phone once again. This time it worked. Sighing with relief he looked around and realised that he had returned to the present. But the strange thing was, he could still see, down the end of the road, people still walking around in 1967.

By this time Sean had seen enough, and dived onto a bus to go home. When he was interviewed by the local newspaper later, he stated over four times, the exact account.

Now, you may think that Sean was making the story up to escape from the guard. But the strange tale didn't end there. When the Security Guard was interviewed, he stated that when he ran after Sean, and turned down the dead end Alley after him, he said that Sean had completely disappeared!

When the newspaper checked out the facts of Sean's story, they found that everything he said was historically accurate.

Technical Analysis

Could this be a strange Quantum effect or Leakage?

I wondered, what if in Quantum physics, **time was not linear—but spiral**. Whereas the centre is the beginning of time and the end point of the outer-rings is the current day. As far as we know, the only thing that can affect time is gravity... the only thing that can affect gravity is mass... and the only things with enough mass to affect gravity are planets. I came up with an idea that maybe when the planets align in certain configurations, their relative positions could have a combined gravitational interaction or push/pull effect that could affect localised spiral timelines. This push/pull affect may be high frequency, but short-term. The result of which is the bending of the current day outer spiral timeline, bringing it closer to the previous ring. As they get too close there could there be an interaction—a **data leak**—between **older lines** to the current. When the old and new rings connect, a paranormal type event occurs as voices, images, and/or a playback of past events are observed. A bit like crosstalk on old analogue TV sets when environmental effects cause the channel 2 broadcast to shadow on channel 1. This made some sense, as the planets would be the timing mechanism to which this effect may occur.

If I modelled historical star patterns with the exact timings and locality of an observed activity—could it be possible to predict if or when this effect would occur again?

In the beginning, my idea felt quite reasonable. It accounted for events I had read about and experienced myself, including the sighting of the monk back home. The monk also seemed to fit the third party reports of ghost observations around the country— ghosts of people walking down the same stairs, **around about** the same times, in the same places. In my mind, I perceived this as a **one-way** projection/quantum crosstalk mechanism.

In effect, an **error of nature** when mass imposes on gravity and gravity imposes on timelines causing shadows of the past; a one-way **quantum error** which has **been misinterpreted by** people into believing it is **interactive.**

But something kept bugging me! The problem was paranormal events **seem to have a clockwork,** but the clock seems to be malfunctioning? I say this as thousands of people witness the same repeating events, the same sightings, and same activity keeps **reoccurring in the same areas.** Yet, the timing **trigger** isn't set; it seems to be random. A good example of this is the Battle of Gettysburg in 1863 Pennsylvania during the American Civil war. Even today people randomly report hearing gunshots and seeing what looks to be ghost solders walking around as if they are replaying the war...

From a technical point of view, this really bothered me. Planets **move** like clockwork. If it was a by-product of gravitation, we would see the same things, at **roughly** the same times, on **roughly** around the same dates when the planets hit certain configurations. In other words, a pattern would emerge and some mathematical genius would have picked up on it by now.

Also, paranormal activity would affect a much broader target with **people everywhere** seeing the **ghosts of the past** at around about the same time **all over the world.** The cold reality is, this isn't happening—my idea was wrong and in the end I concluded this phenomenon could not be related to a planetary timing mechanism or timeline crosstalk. This is the issue with "Time Slip" theory: this paranormal behaviour is too random, but also highly specific and too localised to be a grand error of nature. At this point, I got the feeling something else was at work. Something much more elaborate that I couldn't quite pin down, and maybe, I'm looking at it all wrong... One thing I learnt early on in I.T is "never bend the data to one's idea," rather "...adapt the idea to work with the data."

Argument for: Spirits are Dead Humans

The most favoured idea is that ghosts are *the dead* returning as spirits. Whereby some of the deceased return due to unfinished business, others are lost stuck infinitely wandering and roaming the earth for answers. For those that are stuck here and lost in the tide of time—they are trapped in a loop, stuck haunting the areas of where they perished, or simply don't know they are dead and carry on with life unknowingly. The theory argues that one way these spirits communicate is by manipulating radio waves and sending messages though Spirit Boxes. Indeed, during paranormal investigations these boxes sometimes pick up names that do relate to historical events or names of people who have passed.

Technical Analysis

This is by far the most emotionally romantic idea with many self-proclaimed psychic mediums and TV shows financially benefitting from such beliefs. The fact is, the act these people provide can be replicated and performed better by stage artists. One such artist is Derren Brown.

- Derren Brown is an English mentalist, illusionist, and author. Since his television debut with *Derren Brown: Mind Control* in 2000, Brown has produced several other shows for the stage and television in both series and specials.

This spirits-are-the-deceased idea/belief system has become the **predominate force** within paranormal research. Teams and TV shows call out ghosts **by name,** perceiving that the activity is caused by people that have passed over the years. Indeed, as a teen and into my twenties I had a dog. After he died, I used to hear him walking around the house and scraping on doors. Once I even saw him sitting in his old place by the radiator as I walked in one day.

The problem is **the human element** or in other words our **human nature**: Paranormal behaviour patterns observed during research are not consistent with natural human behaviour. For instance, there is an active location in Apethorn lane Hyde; a tunnel which people relate to the murder of Mr. Thomas Ashton.

Reference: *https://hydonian.blogspot.com/2012/09/the-murder-of-mr-thomas-ashton.html*

On January 3rd, 1831 Thomas Ashton was shot dead as he made his way from his home at Pole Bank to Apethorn Mill. The following report is from the Stockport Advertiser of January 7th, 1831 headed *'HORRIBLE MURDER':*

- *On Monday last one of the most cruel and sanguinary murders which ever disgraced a civilized people, was perpetrated on the body of Mr. Thomas Ashton, eldest son of Samuel Ashton, Esq., of Pole Bank, Werneth, in this parish, so early as seven o'clock in the evening. The victim of this cold-blooded and diabolical act of assassination, who was in his 24th year, and remarkable for his kind and conciliating disposition and manners, had the management of a new mill belonging to his father at Woodley, from whence he had just returned and was on his way to the other mill at Apethorn to superintend for his younger brother, James, who had just left home to spend the evening with a family near Stockport. The father and mother were in the house at the time waiting the return of the carriage to join the brother and the other part of the family who had gone with him, and the effect of so distressing a communication may more easily be imagined than described. It appeared on the examination of the witnesses before the coroner that the unfortunate gentleman had not proceeded on the public highway, after quitting the private road, which leads from Pole Bank to Apethorn Mills, more than 30 yards, before he was shot; and it would appear on examination of the premises about the fatal spot that the assassins had awaited his approach, sitting behind a hedge bank on the road side, which situation gave them the best opportunity of seeing or hearing the approach of their victim from his father's house down the private pathway. The breast was perforated at the edge of the bone by two bullets from a horse pistol or blunderbuss, which had passed out at the left shoulder blade, having taken an oblique direction upwards. His death must have been instantaneous, for when found his right hand was in his greatcoat pocket—a manner of placing it quite usual with him when walking. He was lying in a shallow ditch on the contrary side of the road to the one generally taken by the family when going to the mill, and this is accounted for by the supposition, that he must have retreated to the other side when approached by the assassin in order to avoid him. The muzzle of the weapon appears to have been placed close to his breast, as the wadding perforated his garments, and part of it— some coarse blue paper—had entered his body, and was concealed in the sternum.*"

APETHORN LANE. SCENE OF THE MURDER
OF MR. THOMAS ASHTON.

Even though the active tunnel isn't that close to the murder site, people believe that Thomas Ashton haunts it.

The question begs, why would a man from the 18th century hang around a tunnel at night and only at night?

People have said many times, "if they were a ghost, they would be sightseeing around the world staying in the best hotels for free!" Life (or death) by all accounts would be great! Holding out alone, in a tunnel, all night, in the cold, does not match natural human behaviour. Human beings are generally pack animals who like the interaction of others; holding out in a small tunnel—alone, in woodland doesn't make any sense.

Human behaviour is generally cooperative and information sharing. I have said many a time that if my chatterbox relatives were ghosts they wouldn't stop telling everyone what they can see, or do, etc. They would be leaving everyone messages in one form or another; their new abilities and spirit bodies would be the talk of the town!

Imagine if you had a brilliant grandmother who came back to visit as a ghost. She would love to use these new supernatural abilities to help out around the house! This all sounds great, but sadly, the reality is this level of communication/interaction between the dead and living isn't occurring. Instead what we see are areas/buildings suddenly becoming active—objects thrown about, banging, strange electrical effects, with basic information exchange generally mentioned via EVP – Electronic voice phenomena or other means.

In cold logic, the behaviour patterns simply **don't match**. Why would anyone in spirit form be hanging around a graveyard at 2 am? Or walking about a derelict, rotten old house? Or suddenly start haunting a cellar somewhere?

However, with all of the above mentioned—my personal experience also conflicts with my own questioning. My family once owned a pet parrot. The night he died I heard him flapping and flying around the kitchen as clear as a bell. It was *so* clear that I even checked his cage where his dead body remained.

This experience suggested there could be a **different state** that is still applicable to the laws of physics, but has yet to be defined. In regard to my pet parrot, I also noticed that after that **one evening** I *never* heard it again. This could indicate that there could be a situation when humans or mammals die and can stay, **but only** for short periods of time...

This small window of time **could be responsible** for the reports of **interactive communications** of **passed family members and even animals**. However, in the case of this project the long-term **constant** haunting and activity is the only thing I can reference and test. I believe the findings mentioned in this book is not connected to what mainstream researchers define as **"the spirit world"**, but a totally separate domain which has been **misidentified** as "spirit." I personally believe this separate domain is responsible for 90+ percent of haunting.

"The way we experience the world around us is a direct reflection of the world within us."

Gabrielle Bernstein

PART TWO

OBSERVED PARANORMAL ACTIVITY AND BEHAVIOURS THAT REPLICATE WORLDWIDE

If an **object or function/mechanism** is performing a non-standard /out of place observable **behaviour** or **action in multiple locations** , then it logical to state that function/mechanism is developed by the same **source**. That is, the mechanism is intelligently designed to perform that *specific* task.

During my research, I found a number of common behaviour traits within paranormal activity that are replicated worldwide.

The list is as follows:

EVP - Electronic Voice Phenomenon

Overview of two observable mechanisms

- The first observable mechanism is one of the most common types: audio playback of **out of place/strange/disembodied** voices recorded on digital/tape recorders.

These voices are **not heard** at the time of recording, but on playback; voices that were not present at the time can be heard.

During the British Scole Experiment **1993—1998**

Reference: *https://www.thescoleexperiment.com/the-scole-experiment-overview.html*

- *In 1993, the Scole Experimental Group embarked on a five-year experiment using a revolutionary kind of 'energy' to produce tangible objects from the spirit world. The term 'tangible objects' means things recognisable to our senses or our instruments—visible manifestations, lights, sounds, touches, tastes and smells. Some of the tangible objects took the form of messages transmitted onto photographic film, audio-tape and videotape.*

- *These voices were reproduced inside a **faraday cage;** these cages block all electromagnetic signals. Thus debunking the idea that these EVPs were the products of external radio interference.*

EVP are quite interesting, as researchers can 1) hear intelligent responses to questions they ask; and 2) hear audio playbacks of historic events. An example of this is an EVP saying a short statement such as "the king is dead" or calling a historic name of someone in the past, etc.

The method generally used is a tape or digital recorder. However, these days' mobile phones recordings are also common. The questions are 1) how do these voices get imprinted on the recordings; and 2) how are they created?

The mainstream paranormal community belief-system claims that the spirits communicate in a **frequency outside the range of human hearing.** This idea is technically inaccurate for a number of reasons.

- EVPs can be picked up on basic tape recorders
- Tape has a recording (dynamic range) of 50 to 60db
- Frequency response of 16 to 18Khz

Cross Ref Djinn frequency

If tape is picking this up, then **hearing frequency** has nothing to do with it. In fact, human hearing is even better at 120db dynamic range with a frequency responsive of 20Hz to 20 KHz.

If the tape can pick it up, **why can't we?**

The question becomes, "if it's not frequency, and yet inaudible to human hearing, then how are these voices getting imbedded?"

The second type of EVP that can be heard by the **human ear** itself, these are much rarer but do occur. However, these sound **different** than typical human speech patterns, and are generally more **digital or fuzzy** in nature and much shorter in duration, one could say artificial in nature.

The only way that is possible is with the **compression and expansion/shaping of air.** By creating sound waves—**mimicking the human voice and oral process**—these **sound waves** then travel through the air, vibrating our ear drums, and sending signals to our auditory cortex for processing.

However, there is no observed "**physical being**" to "**compress and shape physical air**"; so *how* can this process occur?

Interestingly, during the Scole Experiments these voices were demonstrated to have been recorded even with the **internal microphone removed** from the recorder itself. In other words, this communication method has **multiple broadcast mechanisms**, which we will cover later in the book.

Black Masses

The most commonly observed ghosts are known as the "**black mass**." These types of ghosts are seen as a 3D solid mass of total blackness that will either stay still or move at speed. Many witness reports state the black mass stands five to six feet tall, are observed predominantly in known active/haunted areas, and point to old buildings such as hospitals, old prisons, and around graveyards. These black masses have been perceived as *monks* over the years.

During these experiences, people claim to feel high anxiety levels *even before* anything had been sighted. Witnesses emotionally encounter repressive feelings and stress in areas where black mass ghosts are active. When in close proximity, these have been observed to be the most active type, throwing objects, banging aggressively, and scratching.

While no one has been reported to be seriously hurt during such encounters, the human reaction *post*-experience is somewhat different, with negative mood changes, including intense anger/rage and/or depression for months. *Temporal lobe reduction effects*

The question bears asking: **What are these?**

Sudden Mood Change: Anxiety

Many times, people and paranormal researchers who have spent long periods inside **haunted / active** areas describe it as the following...

- *"It is comparable to a steam room"*
- *"Fine when you walk in, but as the minutes tick by it feels more suffocating to the point one needs to leave"*
- *"Over time, one becomes more on edge, tense, and claustrophobic"*

Oppressive emotions and feelings of dizziness are common—even memory has been observed to be affected. During my research, I observed genuine people knowingly **close a door** and then moment later ask, **"Who closed it?"**

I have also personally observed people making verbal statements or **moving** objects without memory or reason of having done so.

Could this be some kind of stress related human condition or something else at play?

Possession

Possession is reported all over the world, whereas a person within an active location starts acting *totally out of character*, generally in an aggressive and/or spontaneous manner. Afterward, those affected will have limited memory of actions, and once the person has left the area, the effect disappears—leaving the person feeling distorted, lethargic, and confused.

Many people refer to the case of 21-year-old Elisa Lam, the Canadian woman found dead in the rooftop water tank of the Cecil Hotel in downtown Los Angeles on February 19, 2013.

Reference: *https://www.youtube.com/watch?v=3TjVBpyTeZM*

Elisa Lam

2013 picture of Lam distributed by Los Angeles police

Her body was found naked, with most of her clothes and personal effects floating in the water near her. It took the Los Angeles County Coroner's office *four months* to release the autopsy report. We now know there was no evidence of physical trauma and the manner of death is stated as accidental.

On observing the public domain CCTV footage, the young lady in the elevator (Elisa Lam) appears to be **taken over** while the elevator appeared to be randomly malfunctioning. Appearing to be disturbed, she looks discreetly around the corner of the doors as if something was calling her. During this footage the elevator doors wouldn't close—this is only possible if someone was repeatedly pushing the call button or the elevators IR beam was broken by an unseen force. However, she was reported to have been alone throughout the whole experience.

The question bears asking: *"How could possession be technically possible?"*

Strange Electronic Malfunctions

Electronic devices have been observed to **drain power**, start to randomly fail, or perform badly. A phone will ring and upon answering, there is no one on the other end but **static**. In some cases, the settings have even been changed for no reason...

- Fully charged power cells go dead
- Computers suddenly crash/run badly for no reason
- Cameras switching off randomly and hot to the touch
- Lights flicker as if something is drawing power from the main circuit
- Walkie talkies start acting strange and/or experience power loss

The question bears asking: *"What can cause all these strange effects and why?"*

Full Body or Object Apparition

Some have witnessed **people or objects** (including **animals** and **manufactured objects**) appear and disappear. During these experiences, the objects are perceived as **solid as** they kick up stones and dust as they pass—only then to *vanish* seconds later.

The question bears asking: *"What mechanism could replicate this?"*

Getting Followed

It has also been generally observed that people say that after the initial experience that **something has followed them.** The sensation of being followed can make one uneasy and stressed even in the safely of their own home.

Many researchers find that regardless of how complex one's journey home is, one's home or room will become **semi- active** for a short period of time. While the occupant is in a deep state of relaxation, voices are heard, scratching, tapping on walls, and objects **disappearing** and **reappearing** within the house.

The question bears asking: *"How can paranormal activity follow you?"*

Poltergeist Activity

Poltergeist means "playful or mischievous spirit" *Djinn !*

However, in real life, this activity is impossible to live with long-term.

The observations contain the **constant combinations** of many **smaller actions**:

- Objects thrown
- banging/tapping/scratching on walls and objects
- scratches on people's skin
- disembodied voices heard by human hearing
- EVPs on recorder and phones
- Objects disappearing and reappearing—and found in clear, obvious locations
- Activity can be so intense that the home isn't just **unliveable**— it's **unsellable!**

The question bears asking: *"What are they, for what reason, and why?"*

Buildings That Suddenly Become Active Then Stop

It should be noted that reports of *new homes* and areas have been found to be **active**, while thousands of *old homes* that are hundreds of years-old are **not active**. Then you have other buildings and areas which never had any activity—but suddenly become active for no clear reason.

The question bears asking: *"Why do areas become active and then stop?"*

The Witching Hours

Ingrained in history—between 3 am and 4am—is observed to be the **most active** time of the night.

Reference:
https://en.wikipedia.org/wiki/Witching_hour_(supernatural)

"In folklore, the witching hour or devil's hour is a time of night associated with supernatural events. Creatures such as witches, demons and ghosts are thought to appear and to be at their most powerful. Black magic is thought to be most effective at this time. In the Western Christian tradition, the hour between 3 and 4 a.m. was considered a period of peak supernatural activity, due to the absence of prayers in the canonical hours during this period."

The question bears asking: *"Why this time period?"*

PART THREE

TRADITIONAL AND WIDELY-
ACCEPTED TYPES OF GHOSTS

Type: The Poltergeist

Description: Poltergeists are said to be "noisy ghosts." They have been observed possessing the ability to manipulate their physical environment, such as 1) opening windows; 2) moving chairs; 3) push books off of shelves; 4) randomly turn lights on; and 4) even starting fires.

not only consciously thought" but perceptions

Type: The Interactive Personality

Description: These are said to be the most common ghosts—loved ones who return to convey important information. Interactive personalities are observed to emit a scent such as a perfume or cigarette smoke, in order to help the living sense their presence.

Type: Orbs

Description: Orbs are the most frequently presented photographic evidence said to support the existence of ghosts. They emit different colours—observed as translucent balls of light—that appear to hover over the ground in pictures. Orbs are said to be "the soul of a human or animal" that is travelling from one place to another. The assumption the mainstream paranormal community makes on why they appear as circles is interesting; they claim it's because this shape makes it easier for them to travel around. It is also perceived that the longer they exist in our world, the easier they can transform into full-bodied apparitions. *Path of least resistance – bubbles by nature infolding gravitational pressures to maintain shape*

Type: Funnel Ghosts

Description: These ghosts are perceived as loved ones returning to visit. They are observed frequently in old historical buildings or inside of private homes where they once lived.

Funnel Ghosts are said to cause *cold spots* and when seen, appear as a swirling funnel. They can also be caught in photographs as a spiral of light.

Types: Ectoplasm/Ecto-Mist

Description: These ghosts are said to appear several feet off the ground. They take the shape of a swirling mass of white, grey, or black mist. Observed to move quickly, they can also choose to remain in place and orbit. Ectoplasm/Ecto-Mist is observed mostly outdoors in graveyards, in battlefields, and general historical sites.

Type: Demons

Description: Demons are said to be powerful, supernatural beings. They can invade homes; attach themselves to objects; inflict mental and/or physical torture; and are most commonly witnessed as black masses standing in doorways. The mainstream paranormal community claims these ghosts should never be challenged because they are capable of killing.

Type: Shadow People

Description: Observed as a silhouette of a person, appearing to be wearing a hood or a cloak, observed to walk through walls.

Type: Animal Ghosts

Description: Observed to appear as full-body apparitions, animal ghosts are said to be commonly heard rather than seen. Scratching on the doors or on walls, make scraping sounds against the floor, whining, and/or barking is said to be reported.

Type: Inanimate Ghosts

Description: Said to be "residual," this type of ghost is said to take the form of physical objects such as cars, trains, or a horse-and-cart. Inanimate Ghosts are defined as a playback of time via **left over energy.** *Stone-tape hypothesis?*

Type: Doppelgänger

Description: These ghosts are said to project themselves in multiple places at once, and even mimic the look of someone who is still living. People have stated they see someone they know, but in reality, that person is in a completely different location.

Reference: *https://www.ghostsandgravestones.com/types-of-ghosts*

A Brief History

The paranormal has been consistently researched since the 1800s; most of which formulated the above definitions. The following is a brief history:

- 1817: an unknown scientist investigated the reported ghostly happenings at the Tower of London.

- 1830: Marie Laveau (a Louisiana Creole practitioner of Voodoo) gains the title "Voodoo Queen" of New Orleans in the 1830s. She was born in 1801.

- 1833: Michael Banim published his fictional novel titled, "The Ghost-Hunter and His Family."

- 1834: Major Edward Moor investigated the Great Bealings House.

- 1837: The Georgian era ends, and the Victorian era begins this year (and ended in 1901).

- 1840: Dr. Edward Drury (a physician) of Sunderland investigated a reportedly haunted house in 1840 at Willington Mill, near Newcastle. The mill was owned by Joseph Proctor (a Quaker). Drury was called a "ghost detector" in the January 1860 edition of "The Spiritual Magazine."

- 1848: The Fox Sisters, who lived in what was then Hydesville, NY, (now called Lily Dale) have been often credited for ushering in the beginning of The Spiritualist Movement. Some argue that The Spiritualist Movement started before the Fox sisters (see the book "Spiritualism: A Popular History From 1847" by Joseph McCabe, page 10, published in 1920. I have one of the original copies of this book, very interesting read). Kate (Catherine) Fox and Maggie (Margaret) Fox were mediums who took their show on the road. The third sister, Leah Fox, operated as their manager. Their career ended in 1888, when Maggie admitted to hoaxing. Later, Maggie withdrew her "confession" saying that she lied when she said

Minor neurons nonetheless?

they hoaxed it. Whether Maggie did any hoaxing is anyone's guess. However, many people witnessed the phenomena at the Fox house even when Maggie was nowhere around.

- 1853: Michael Faraday (yes, that Faraday) conducted experiments with table-turning in 1853.

- 1859: The book titled "Footfalls of the Boundary of another World" written by psychical researcher Robert Dale Owen (a strong believer in Spiritualism) was published this year, 528 pages.

- 1861: Sir William Crookes (a chemist and physicist) conducted his first paranormal investigation by testing the medium, Kate Fox (one of the famous 'Fox Sisters' of the Spiritualist Movement, see 1848). Crookes went on in later years to investigate the mediums Florence Cook and Daniel Dunglas Home.

- 1862: The Ghost Club was officially founded in 1862 in London, England, but has its roots in a discussion group at Cambridge University in 1855. Members of The Ghost Club included Charles Dickens, Siegfried Sassoon, Harry Price, Donald Campbell, Peter Cushing, Peter Underwood, Maurice Grosse, Sir Shane Leslie and Eric Maple. It is still in existence today.

- 1871: Sir William Crookes began testing the medium, Daniel Douglas Home, which lasted two years. Daniel was also popular for his reported ability to levitate. It is said he "floated" out a window then "floated" back in through another window on the third floor of Lord Adare's home in 1868 in London, England. Other reports of his levitation demonstrations exist.

- 1874: Sir William Crookes began testing the medium, Florence Cook.

- 1881: Harry Price was born on Jan 17, 1881. On June 16, 1881 Marie Laveau (Voodoo Queen) dies in New Orleans at the age of 80.

- 1882: The Society for Psychical Research was founded in London in 1882 by Henry Sidgwick, Frederic Myers, and Edmund Gurney. Henry Sidgwick was the first President of The Society for Psychical Research. Members have included William Barrett, Lord Rayleigh, Arthur Balfour, and Gerald Balfour. It is still in existence today. Their website states that they are "the first organisation established to examine allegedly paranormal phenomena using scientific principles."

- 1884: The American Society for Psychical Research was founded in 1884. Members have included Sigmund Freud, Carl G. Jung, and Alexander Graham Bell. It also is still in existence today.

- 1890: The patent for the Ouija board (a type of spirit board) was filed on May 28, 1890, and the patent was issued on Feb 10, 1891.

- 1891: The book titled "Revelations of a Spirit Medium," which exposed the tricks of fake psychics, was written this year by an anonymous author named 'A Medium.' This book was later reprinted and edited by Harry Price and Eric J. Dingwall in 1922. This was also one of the books that inspired magician Harry Houdini to take up the duty of exposing fake psychics in the early 1920s.

Also, William Thomas Stead (a pioneer of investigative journalism) wrote the book titled "Real Ghost Stories" published in 1891. Eerily, in 1892 he wrote a fictional story about a ship that collided with an iceberg — twenty years later Stead died aboard the infamous Titanic. But his wasn't the only "prediction" of the Titanic.

Reference: https://coldspot.org/2013/11/08/history-ghost-hunting-1800s/

Current day

As of now paranormal research has never been so popular. On YouTube alone the video count is incredible with thousands of small research groups making content every day. Each week public groups are heading out and observing Poltergeist type activity and yet, even with all this **research time,** the paranormal community is the first to admit that they have hit a wall of confusion.

Confusion, contradictory logic, or jumbled ideas have the general public defaulting back to the basic idea that they are interacting with dead humans.

As previously mentioned the only way this belief system can continue to exist is by cherry-picking very loose ideas and ignoring huge counter arguments. This is unfortunate, because in reality the only way to find out the truth is by taking *all* known facts into account to cut away the dead wood and find out what's going on.

One of these **counter arguments** is a numerical problem—I call this…

PART FOUR

THE MATHEMATICAL DILEMMA
OF GHOSTS

They say that mathematics is the **science of logical reasoning;** let's apply it to statistical data of recorded human deaths worldwide and known areas of paranormal activity. By this method we can quickly see if there is a mathematical correlation or not. If there is, we can all sigh a breath of relief; we might have some hard data that **life continues after death**. But if the numbers are way out, it means something else could be at work… So let's get to it!

According to the "Our World in Data" run by the "Global Change Data Lab"

https://ourworldindata.org/births-and-deaths -

In 2015

- Overall 57 million people died
- 156,164 people died each day
- 6,506 people died each hour
- 108 people died each minute

The reality is these numbers are large; if you take that 57 million number and times it by 10 (ten year period) that number jumps to **five hundred & seventy million** every decade. Yet, with the high numbers of deaths, paranormal activity seems to remain at a low level. There are still reports of it occurring, but it's reasonably rare.

Many people say that the calculations are *impossible* to work out but the reality is—it is not...

So, how can we work this out?

- If just one percent of people who died (57 million) came back as ghosts, that's 570,000 (or five-hundred and seventy thousand) new ghosts every year—year-in year-out.
- Over a 50 year period: 570,000 ghosts x 50 years = 28,500,000 (or twenty-eight million five-hundred thousand) new ghosts

But for the sake of argument, let's reduce that even lower to 0.1%...

- That's 57,000 (fifty-seven thousand) new ghosts every year
- Every decade that's 570,000 (five-hundred and seventy thousand) new ghosts
- Every century that's 5,700,000 (five million seven-hundred thousand) new ghosts

While some haunting have been observed to last for years, with some locations active for many decades.

The question bears asking: *"Where are they all?"*

Mathematically, even at a tiny return rate of 0.1% we should be inundated—the reality is **"we are not"**. Paranormal activity isn't common but it from my own experiences it does appear to be real but it seems to remain at the same low but never the less consistent rate.

The paranormal community argument states only the ones who have **unfinished business** come back, but the sad reality is a **lot more** than 0.1% of the human population have unfinished business or pass in a sudden unexpected event.

- For example: according to new figures from the Centers for

Disease Control and Prevention, a steady rise in suicides involving firearms has pushed the rate of gun deaths in the US to its highest rate in more than 20 years. Almost 40,000 people were killed in shootings in 2017. **According to the mainstream paranormal thought process,** 2017 should have been the most active period in 20 years with 40,000 new spirits roaming around... but nothing changed.

- In a way, the terrible events of 911 were a great example of this; 3,000 people died in **one** attack in **one** area at **one** time presumably all **with unfinished business** *and* all died in a very distressed sudden way. However, downtown NYC isn't flooded with paranormal activity and the new Freedom Tower isn't haunted with the ghosts of 3,000 people.

The interesting fact is the bulk of the paranormal community and research groups **refuse to acknowledge these logical arguments.** The bubble remains intact, the religion remains unquestioned; the same echo chambers remain. The reason for this disassociation could be because people **generally relate** their perceptions to an earthly answer—something they can relate to **which makes people feel comfortable** in the face of a very unusual phenomena.

When a new haunting starts, the general process of events generally unrolls like this:

- An area and building suddenly become active
- The owners start complaining and the story goes public
- The media pushes it out
- The researches rush in and start reading the history books

The case of 30 East Drive Pontefract is known as **the most aggressive Poltergeist in Europe.** Researchers dug back 500 years to find one story that barely fits. A monk was killed there - must be him!

But the reality is you would be lucky to find a bit of land **anywhere** where someone hasn't died or been killed at some point in its documented history.

The London Underground is a perfect example. During construction many graves were dug through and more recently archaeologists had to dig up **60,000 ancient skeletons** for the excavation for the HS3 High Speed rail link. This entire disturbance of graves and yet London underground isn't haunted to the brim; yes, there are reports of small minor paranormal activities, but overall nothing is going on.

Once again the current mainstream belief system can *only* exist by cherry-picking very loose ideas while ignoring many counter arguments. This was understandable back in the 16th or 18th century where science was in its infancy. Now we are a high-technology, near space-faring civilisation and it's time to re-examine this with a fresh pair of eyes.

PART FIVE

THE NOISY DEFENCE CONTRACTOR

During my research, what recently stood out was a statement from Lockheed Martin's senior research scientist—Boyd Bushman.

Background

The following is a list of Bushman's patents published throughout
his career ↳ Lockheed . *Senior research Scientist*

- System and method for electromagnetic propulsion fan, patent
number: 6606578 *based on Schist Disk?. Look into* ✱
- Variable ratio angled magnetic drive, patent number: 6411001
- Method and apparatus for detecting emitted radiation from
interrupted electrons:, patent number: 6028434
- Plume or combustion detection by time sequence
differentiation of images over a selected time interval, patent
number: 5999652
- Metal detection system and process using a high voltage to
produce a visible electrical discharge, patent number: 5982180
- Apparatus and method for amplifying a magnetic beam, patent
number: 5929732 △
- Airfoil leading edge with cavity, patent number: 5836549
- Plume or combustion detection by time sequence
differentiation, patent number: 5793889
- Aircraft engine nozzle, patent number: 5775635
- Method and apparatus for filter infrared emission, patent
number: 5726798 *Kirlian reverse?*
- Radiation communication system, patent number: 5680135 *ET Communer*
- Thermally energized electrical power source, patent number:
5637946
- Apparatus powered using laser supplied energy, patent number:
5542247
- Power transfer apparatus and method, patent number: 5514926 *dirty?*
- Detection system, patent number: 5504486 *wtf*
- Position identification device using an accelerometer, patent
number: 5492010
- Object detection system, patent number: 5430448

- Heat radiation detection system, patent number: 5428221
- Wave attenuation, patent number: 5420588
- Laser apparatus, patent number: 5384802

A brief review of Lockheed Martin

Lockheed Martin is an American global aerospace, defence, security and advanced technologies company with worldwide interests. It was formed by the merger of Lockheed Corporation with Martin Marietta in March 1995. It is headquartered in Bethesda, Maryland, in the Washington DC area. Lockheed Martin employs approximately 100,000 people worldwide.

Lockheed Martin is one of the largest companies in the aerospace, defence, security, and technologies industry. It is the world's largest defence contractor based on revenue for fiscal year 2014. In 2013, 78% of Lockheed Martin's revenues came from military sales; it topped the list of US federal government contractors and received nearly 10% of the funds paid out by the Pentagon. In 2009, US government contracts accounted for $38.4 billion (85%), foreign government contracts $5.8 billion (13%), and commercial and other contracts for $900 million (2%). Lockheed Martin operates in four business segments: Aeronautics, Missiles and Fire Control, Rotary and Mission Systems, and Space Systems. The company has received the Collier Trophy six times, including in 2001 for being part of developing the X-35/F-35B Lift Fan Propulsion System, and most recently in 2006 for leading the team that developed the F-22 Raptor fighter jet. Lockheed Martin is currently developing the F-35 Lightning II and leads the international supply chain, leads the team for the development and implementation of technology solutions for the new USAF Space Fence (AFSSS replacement), and is the primary contractor for the development of the Orion (spacecraft) command module.[12] The company also invests in healthcare systems, renewable energy systems, intelligent energy distribution and compact nuclear fusion.

Reference: *https://en.wikipedia.org/wiki/Lockheed_Martin*

Projects include

Lockheed D-21 - The Lockheed D-21 is a supersonic, reconnaissance drone. The D-21 was initially designed to be launched from the back of a M-21 carrier aircraft, a variant of the Lockheed A-12 aircraft. In the 1960s Lockheed's secret Skunk Works developed the Mach 3 A-12 reconnaissance aircraft for the Central Intelligence Agency (CIA). After the shooting down of the U-2 piloted by Gary Powers in 1960, a number of different concepts were proposed as alternatives. Kelly Johnson, the leader of Skunk Works, developed the concept of a long-range drone that used much of the A-12's technology. In October 1962 the CIA and the United States Air Force (USAF) instructed Lockheed to study a high-speed, high-altitude drone concept. Johnson specified speeds of Mach 3.3–3.5, an operational altitude of 87,000–95,000 feet (27,000–29,000 m), and a range of 3,000 nautical miles (3,500 mi; 5,600 km). It was intended to make a one-way trip, eject its camera payload at the end of the mission for recovery, then self-destruct.[2] It had a double-delta wing similar to the A-12's wing design. The Q-12 was to be air-launched from the back of an A-12, and used key technology from the A-12 Project, including titanium construction and radar cross-section reduction design features.

Reference:

DAYTON, Ohio -- Lockheed D-21B at the National Museum of the United States Air Force. (U.S. Air Force photo)

The Lockheed F-117 Nighthawk is an single-seat, twin-engine stealth attack aircraft that was developed by Lockheed's secretive Skunk Works division and operated by the United States Air Force. The Nighthawk was the first operational aircraft to be designed around stealth technology. Its maiden flight took place in 1981, and the aircraft achieved initial operating capability status in 1983. The Nighthawk was shrouded in secrecy until it was revealed to the public in 1988. Of the 64 F-117s built, 59 were production versions, with the other five being demonstrators/prototypes. These craft were the precursor to the B2 Stealth built by Northrop Grumman.

The F-117 was widely publicized for its role in the Persian Gulf War of 1991. Although it was commonly referred to as the "Stealth Fighter", it was strictly an attack aircraft. F-117s took part in the conflict in Yugoslavia, where one was shot down by a surface-to-air missile (SAM) in 1999; it was the only Nighthawk to be lost in combat. The U.S. Air Force retired the F-117 in 2008, primarily due to the fielding of the F-22 Raptor.

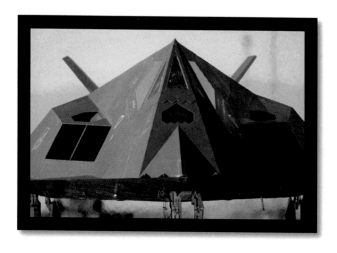

The **Blackbird** is a long-range, Mach 3+ strategic reconnaissance aircraft that was operated by the United States Air Force.

It was developed as a black project from the Lockheed A-12 reconnaissance aircraft in the 1960s by Lockheed and its Skunk Works division. American aerospace engineer Clarence "Kelly" Johnson was responsible for many of the design's innovative concepts. During aerial reconnaissance missions, the SR-71 operated at high speeds and altitudes to allow it to outrace threats. If a surface-to-air missile launch were detected, the standard evasive action was simply to accelerate and outfly the missile. The SR-71 was designed with a reduced radar cross-section.

The SR-71 served with the U.S. Air Force from 1964 to 1998. A total of 32 aircraft were built; 12 were lost in accidents, but none were lost to enemy action. The SR-71 has been given several nicknames, including "Blackbird" and "Habu." It has held the world record for the fastest air-breathing manned aircraft since 1976; this record was previously held by the related Lockheed YF-12.

Reference: Lockheed M-21 carrier (SR-71 Blackbird) and D-21 drone, Seattle Museum Of Flight, Washington/2006

Lockheed Martin F-22A Raptor is a fifth-generation, single-seat, twin-engine, all-weather stealth tactical fighter aircraft developed for the United States Air Force. The result of the USAF's Advanced Tactical Fighter program, the aircraft was designed primarily as an air superiority fighter, but also has ground attack, electronic warfare, and signal intelligence capabilities. The prime contractor, Lockheed Martin, built most of the F-22's airframe and weapons systems and conducted final assembly, while Boeing provided the wings, aft fuselage, avionics integration, and training systems. The aircraft was variously designated F-22 and F/A-22 before it formally entered service in December 2005 as the F-22A. After a protracted development and despite operational issues, the USAF considers the F-22 critical to its tactical air power, and says that the aircraft is unmatched by any known or projected fighter. The Raptor's combination of stealth, aerodynamic performance, and situational awareness gives the aircraft unprecedented air combat capabilities.

*Reference: Airwolfhound from Hertfordshire, UK:
https://commons.wikimedia.org/wiki/File:F22_Raptor_-
_RIAT_2016_(28422712746).jpg*

Reference: USAF Senior Airman Kaylee Dubois

Boyd Bushman was also one of the very few scientists who appeared to have clearance to speak to reporters. During one of these interviews he performed a **levitation demonstration** using nothing more than 250 turns of number 3 wire, once plugged into main electricity - the coil levitated. He went on to mention *"that by modifying the voltage and the frequency this configuration might well fly and in fact should fly"* The side effect of this configuration is that it's highly dangerous and generates excess heat very fast.

Some interesting events…

November 11, 1987

"Ed Walters, a successful builder and contractor in Gulf Breeze, Florida, noticed an unusual glow behind the thirty-foot pine tree in his yard. He stepped outside to what seemed like a scene from a Spielberg movie. Except it was real. Hovering overhead in eerie silence was a large, glowing, bluish gray craft. Ed stared in disbelief and ran for his Polaroid camera. Knees trembling, he moved quickly, aiming his camera at the pulsing, throbbing mass of energy. Bang! Something hit him. He couldn't move. Encompassed in a blue light beam, he was lifted from the ground. Rapid visions. Strange voices. No air. Panic. Then nothing. He was back on the ground. The blue light was gone. The craft had disappeared. But Ed had the pictures."

"In the weeks that followed, additional sightings were shared by Ed's wife and family and corroborated by hundreds of residents in the Gulf Breeze area. The amazingly clear, close-up photographs presented in the subsequent book, The Gulf Breeze UFO Sightings

were authenticated by professional photographic analysts, including an optical physicist with the U.S. Navy, and by top technical experts with the Polaroid Corporation. Together with Ed and Frances Walters' riveting first-hand account, they provide the most stunning and persuasive UFO evidence to date."

Reference: *http://hybridsrising.com/Articles/Hybrids-Rising-Ed-GulfBreeze-Art.html*

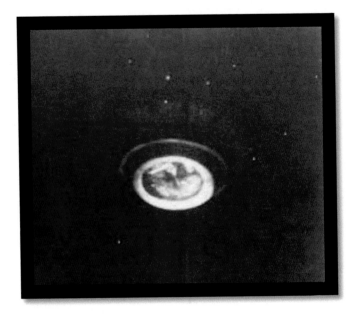

- During Boyd's **levitation demonstration** the coil got very hot and could only be powered for a few seconds before it started burning
- Note the underside centre of its configuration—**a white hot circular parameter.** Could this be the same coil system held inside a vacuum preventing it from burning up?

Boyd concluded that these objects were **probably** man-made and he **might** have been involved at some point in their development. What stands out is the light on top on the craft; it seems to be of low-technology and put on as an afterthought. This is typical in black budget/experimental programs as requirements can change last minute. The engineers will take an existing bit of hardware and perform a rush job it on, after all experimental crafts are used as a technology demonstrator and cosmetics are not that important. Take a close look at the object below—the design of the windows appears to be modular—meaning separate sections have been forged and then installed into the main body. This is the same build process as traditional seafaring ship building.

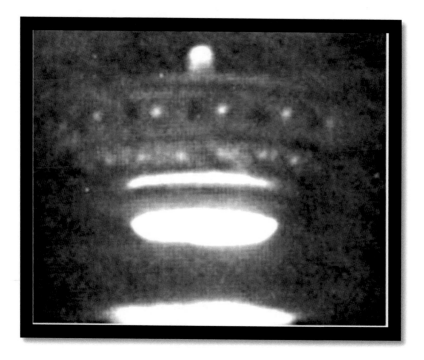

Saturday 12th November 1988

Below is a diagram of one of three crafts that was on display at US Norton Air Force Base during an air show. The three crafts were witnessed by a Mr.Brad Sorenson, who had accidently joined a group of VIPs. The VIP group was taken to a hanger that was off limits to the public. They were told these were Alien Reproduction Vehicles (ARVs) that were under development. Mark McCandlish was an illustrator for the aerospace industry used the information to produce a detailed cross-sectional drawing of the ARV and calculated this craft weighted approx 200 tons.

Reference: Image and render by Mark McCandlish

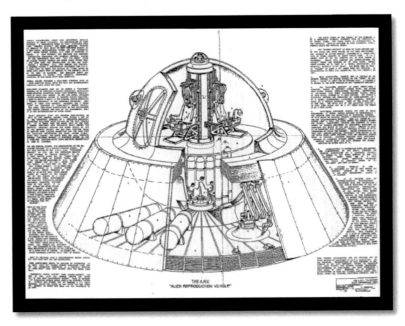

Rendered

February 2001 to March 2002

British hacker Gary McKinnon managed to access NASA/Pentagons central computer file system over this 13-month period looking for free energy technologies.

Reference: http://www.openminds.tv/what-did-ufo-hacker-really-find/3107

Reference: *Gary McKinnon leaves the High Court in London on July 14, 2009. PHOTO: SANG TAN/AP*

McKinnon found a huge security flaw in U.S. computer networks. All of the PCs were built using the same image with a blank administrator password; meaning anyone on the internal network could access these machines unhindered. During his file search, McKinnon found an excel spreadsheet file called *Non-Terrestrial Officers*. It included ranks, names, and had a second tab called *Material Transfers* with a list of 8 to 10 ships. One ship was called the *USSS Hillenkoetter*;

Admiral Roscoe **Hillenkoetter** was the first director of the CIA and was a member of a UFO research organization called the National Investigations Committee on Aerial Phenomena (NICAP). Alleged secret documents that were leaked to UFO researchers list Admiral Hillenkoetter as a member of the infamous Majestic 12 group—an organization rumoured to have been made up of high-ranking military officers and civilians that was supposedly created by President Truman to initially manage the UFO issue.

Admiral Roscoe Hillenkoetter

Reference:

[http://www.nationalufocenter.com/artman/publish/article_415.php
nationalufocenter.com] | Author = US Gov. | Date = 1957

Wednesday, May 9th, 2001

Over twenty military, intelligence, government, corporate and scientific witnesses came forward at the National Press Club in Washington, DC to establish the reality of UFOs or extra-terrestrial vehicles, extra-terrestrial life forms, and resulting advanced energy and
propulsion technologies. The weight of this first-hand testimony,
along with supporting government documentation and other evidence, will establish without any doubt the reality of these phenomena.

This was to be known as the disclosure project...

https://www.disclosureproject.org/

Boyd's levitation coil demonstration and comments regarding the Gulf Breeze, Florida ufos that shared the same propulsion configuration - indicated he was deeply involved in **ARV development** (Alien Reproduction Vehicles).

An Alien Reproduction Vehicle is an earth based-attempt of replicating an extra-terrestrial craft, developed deep within the black budget world of US defence contractors. These projects **are said** to be responsible for the *trillions* of dollars that go missing within the US defence budget. ARVs are said to outperform typical earthbound fighter jets but technically inferior to the objects they were based on.

Between 1998 and the end of fiscal year 2015

PROFESSOR FINDS $21 TRILLION IN UNAUTHORIZED GOVERNMENT SPENDING

By: Gaia Staff

"A Michigan State University economics professor has discovered $21 trillion unaccounted for in the federal budget starting in until 1998 the end of fiscal year 2015. Professor Mark Skidmore enlisted the help of his graduate students to examine government documents from the Department of Defense and Housing and Urban Development to uncover an unfathomable amount of unauthorized spending. According to the Constitution, all federal spending must be voted on and authorized by Congress each fiscal year. Any discrepancies found in the way of unauthorized spending would normally elicit a congressional hearing and investigation.

Skidmore and his students' analysis used publicly available government documents from the two agencies' websites to expose this inconsistency. Shortly after Skidmore published his findings, both agencies removed those documents from public access.

While no congressional committee tied to the budget has opened an inquiry related to Skidmore's findings, the Department of Defence has now said it will conduct its first ever department-wide independent audit.

Skidmore says that sometimes there can be discrepancies meant to account for inadequate transactions, but those adjustments are usually no more than 1 percent of the total budget. The Army's annual budget for FY 2015 was $122 billion, meaning that an adjustment for inadequate transactions might be around $1.2 billion. The Army's actual adjustments for FY 2015 were $6.5 trillion—54 times what it was authorized to spend.

Out of thousands of documents spanning that period, Skidmore was able to find Army budget documentation for 13 of those years, saying its budget represented roughly $11.5 trillion of the missing $21 trillion. He also called these accounting documents "opaque," saying it was not clear what the unauthorized adjustments were for. That amount of unauthorized, "missing" money is equivalent to about $65,000 for every person in America. The government has estimated that the federal deficit sits at around $20 trillion, an entire $1 trillion less than what Skidmore found to be missing in these adjustments.

So, what exactly is this money going towards? The recent revelation of a $56 billion Pentagon black budget for secret military, space, and surveillance programs has led some to speculate that it could be merely a fraction of what's actually being spent.

Skidmore said he reached out to the Office of Inspector General, the Government Accountability Office, and Congressional Budget Office, asking if maybe the $6.5 trillion figure was a mistake and was instead supposed to be $6.5 billion. It was confirmed that $6.5 *trillion was the correct adjustment. Though, when he asked if any of these agencies were alarmed or considering this to be a red flag, his questions were met with slight confusion and little concern. Though Skidmore has reserved his speculation as to what he thinks the money might be going toward, it's clear that either someone knows that a large amount of taxpayer dollars is being spent without authorized permission, or the accounting practices of those in charge of massive amounts of public money are that flawed."*

Reference: *https://www.gaia.com/article/21-trillion-missing-us-budget*

The question one should ask is *"Are these huge sums of money getting spent on ARV technology?"*

Saturday, June 23rd, 2018

A huge announcement was made...

US President Donald Trump announced he was directing the pentagon to create the US Space force.

That is, a US space fleet as an independent service branch, *if* the above is correct. The reality is the US Space Force (USSF) has been in service/development for years. This was a clever move by President Trump as by creating an official independent service; these deep black projects could finally start going public under one command. This is an important move as everything becomes accountable within one official military branch. In the world of black projects command fragmentation can become problematic - who commands access to what technology? Who controls access to what data?

Questions arise - could someone in this shadow world be illegally leaking data to 3rd parties for huge sums of cash? Where has all the money been spent? The very nature of the secrecy can create an oppressive if not corrupt environment.

Wednesday, 8th October 2014

On the 8th October 2014 a video was posted on YouTube - Boyd Bushman did an interview with aerospace engineer Mark Q. Patterson where he referenced two *groups*

"The Wranglers and the Rustlers"

Quote:

"They divide them into two groups. One group are wranglers, and the others are rustlers — the ones who are stealers of cattle. The two groups act differently. The ones that are wranglers are much friendlier, and have a better relationship with us"

As I expected, not much was mentioned in the mainstream media. But I personally felt Boyd was referring to something *bigger* than expected. I wondered if there **was any connection** or **relation** between his statement and what the **general public** call *"paranormal* *activity"* or *"ghosts"*. It was a long shot, but something kept bugging me to try and understand - could there be a bigger picture to this? Is there something going on that we are not aware of? That could justify spending trillions on a space force?

Boyd sadly died at 78 years old in August 2014, with the video released after - leaving us all to pick up the pieces and see what sense we can make of it. Although I wasn't lucky enough to meet Boyd while he was alive, I hope the work presented in this book brings a smile to his face as what is about to be presented is something **- I believe - he has known about for a very long time.**

"Truth is the torch that gleams through the
fog without dispelling it."

Claude Adrien Helvetius

So how do we approach this subject?

The key is a process called reverse engineering - figuring out the connection (if any) between the UFO subject and ghost encounters/paranormal activity.

Reverse engineering, also known as back engineering, is the process by which a man-made object is deconstructed to reveal its designs, architecture, or to extract knowledge from the object. Breaking something down in order to understand it, build a copy or improve it. ... A process that was originally applied only to hardware, reverse-engineering is now applied to software, databases and even human DNA.

As previously discusses, there are a number of ways that can be achieved, in software applications one can decompile the code access the database and work it line by line, however if one does not have access to that level - you need to figure out the systems **behaviour** - one can do this by observing it's default **actions.** These sets of **behaviours** and **actions** create **results** these results are called **signatures,** though observational testing it's possible to work out the **architecture** of a system or process - its logic and rules it abides by. From there we can come to a **logical conclusion** of its **reason...**

Within the paranormal we have a **set of behaviours and types of electrical effects that are observed all around the world**—so first I needed to find a ghost and observe these parameters.

PART SIX

THE MOST COMMON TOOLS PARANORMAL INVESTIGATORS USE

So let's start at the beginning and break it down

The most common tools paranormal investigators use are a mix of the really old to the new and interesting. The most common tool is the **EMF detector** (Electromagnetic Magnetic Field); these are the standard devices used to find strange energy spikes in buildings/areas. From personal experience, the paranormal community **do appear to receive** readings from these devices in areas where no electrical power is present and many people claim to have interactive detentions. Generally one would ask a question and the device would flash once for yes and twice for no.

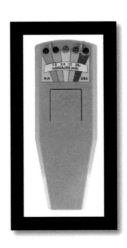

Digital Recorder

Digital recorders are used to document **Electronic Voice Phenomena (EVP).** EVP are strange voices and words from unknown sources that are not audible to the human ear at the time of recording. Only heard during the playback of a recording, the paranormal community perceive EVP as the voices of spirits

Portable Night-Vision Cameras & Full Spectrum Cameras

By using infrared light (IR) that is invisible to human sight, these cameras can **see** in the dark with clarity. Night vision cameras can also pick up anything reflective, such as dust floating around the environment; these dust reflections can be misidentified as orbs.

While Full Spectrum cameras are standard cameras which have had a lens modification to block visible light, thus *only* allowing ultraviolet and infrared light. In effect, full spectrum cameras allows a greater bandwidth of light to be visible than above.

These devices are all very nice, but they all have issues. EMF detectors are triggered by anything that emits electromagnetic waves, including but not limited to 1) mobile phones sending messages or calls; 2) walkie-talkie radio sets; 3) TVs/microwave ovens; and 4) even passing aircrafts. I thought to myself, *"I can't use this as a reliable point of reference as they are just too open for error."* So, I had to find something else.

Digital recorders are interesting, but hearing strange voices or sounds doesn't help to build a dataset to support the reverse engineering process of this phenomena. Night Vision IR and Full-spectrum cameras are helpful, but other than creating video footage, one can't create a dataset. This is all qualitative evidence (categories and impressions); I am looking for quantitative evidence (counted, expressed, and measured) that is based on fact and logic rather than perception and opinion. So what's left?

After hunting around, I saw the paranologies.com custom **Triboelectric field meter.** This meter visually tracks static electricity fields vertically, allowing you to be informed of the direction the field is travelling. This became my device of choice combined with visual analyses; the key was to observe paranormal activity up close and personal, thus being able to observe traits, behaviours, and other physical signatures.

I managed to borrow a Triboelectric field meter from a friend and ran some tests. Inside these units there is a static detector that has quite a high noise floor meaning only very strong static fields are registered

To my surprise they were quite hard to trigger; there was zero reaction to mobile phones or walkie talkies, I even waved my hands around and nothing much happened. At one point I got it to flash but it was only for a moment which is expected as by flapping my arms directly above the unit - with my clothes were generating static it was no supprise the unit started lighting up...

A few days later I got in contact with the owner and developer at "Paranologies", a US based company. He introduced himself as "Mr. Jeromy Jones"—an electronic engineering graduate. Jones was inspired by his father who used to perform séances within his home while he was a child. After a chat about the sensitivity, I ordered a number of them and began to think through how to test them.

PART SEVEN

TAKING ON THE MOST AGGRESSIVE GHOST IN EUROPE

During my research, I found a location known as "30 East Drive" that is said to be "the Black monk house." This location was recognised to be one of the most haunted houses in the UK. The house was small, which is in my favour. Activity (if any) would be localised and observable, unlike say, a huge Castle—where you may experience a bit of activity over a very large area. This localised activity was perfect for up close analysis.

*Back Story—**Reference:** http://www.30eastdrive.com/happenings/*

"Jean, Joe, Phillip (15) and Diane (12) Pritchard moved into Number 30 East Drive, Pontefract in August 1966. Almost immediately, during the hot summer Bank Holiday, Phillip and his Grandmother first witnessed a baffling phenomenon—a fine layer of chalk like dust falling not from the ceiling, but from a level below head height. In an effort to clean up before Phillip's holidaying parents returned, Mrs Kelly (Phillip's Aunty who had been fetched by her mother to observe the falling dust) went to the kitchen for some cleaning implements, whereupon she slipped on a pool of water that had mysteriously appeared. Her efforts to mop up the water were thwarted by more pools appearing on the linoleum in front of her and Phillip's very eyes. This was the beginning of several years of incredible, inexplicable events; green foam appearing from taps and toilet even after the water was turned off, the tea dispenser being activated resulting in all the dried tea cascading onto the work surface, lights being turned off and on, plants leaping out of their pots and landing on the stairs, cupboards shaking violently, photographs being slashed with a sharp knife and an endless list of levitating and thrown objects—including a solid oak sideboard. Dubbed 'Mr Nobody' by the local press in 1968, the family preferred to refer to the poltergeist simply as 'Fred', perhaps as a way of normalising 'It' as no number of initiatives could persuade the entity to leave the family in peace and house-proud mother Jean refused to be terrorised out of her house by an entity. Exorcisms were met with indignation; walls would seep holy water, faces were slapped, people were shoved down the stairs and 'Fred's' hands would appear from nowhere and conduct the Christian songs aimed at showing him off—whilst wearing huge women's fur gloves. In fact, many of Fred's antics were both amazing and often highly amusing, like when he calmly poured an entire jug of milk he removed from the fridge over a sceptical aunt, leaving the kids in stitches. Ordinarily poltergeists aren't known for causing grievous bodily harm, and although Fred caused a few bruises and scrapes

and lot of heart stopping scares, in particular to Diane—seemingly the focus of the haunting—it is rare for a poltergeist to become excessively violent and cause physical harm. But in the case of Fred, that indeed became the case. Late on in his residency, when both Phillip and Diane were beginning to exit adolescence, the activity reached a new climactic height with Diane's long hair suddenly standing on its end, followed by her being dragged kicking and screaming up the stairs, an event that left her seriously traumatised and with clearly visible finger marks on her throat."

30 East Drive" currently operates as a guest house for people to experience the activity up close and personal.

In early 2015 I connected with a couple of camera men—Michael and Steve—who were both interested in this subject. I figured it was best to document everything so I could work though it bit by bit at a later date. Later that day, I contacted the owners and paid to stay for four nights.

The following image is of one of the two cameramen Mike Postlewaite. After experiencing 30 East Drive, Mike started his own paranormal Show, *"Ultimate Haunted UK."*

This plan was simple— **if this haunting was real then maybe** I could trigger it and run a number of tests? In my mind, every time I measured or observed a **reaction,** the **patterns and behaviours I was looking for** would be revealed—the very things I needed to work it out. Like all things when one needs to figure out a mystery, you first need to see the pieces; observe how the game plays; figure out the rules while constantly looking for the chink in the armour. And like all illusions—once you spot that chink, that specific bit of information—the game is all but over as the trick untangles in front of you.

As this was my first time really looking into this, I sat down and thought about the possible issues this would create. I was always hearing about something following you home and causing all sorts of problems with family and friends, etc. This location was reported to be the most aggressive in the UK if not the world. If this was in fact true, I didn't mind putting myself in harm's way, but I didn't want to expose anyone else to this. After all at the time I had no idea what the source or cause of the activity could be and/or how to deal with it.

A couple of weeks, before my stay I went home to see the family and prepped my head. I wanted to ground myself and clear my mind as much as possible. I reminded myself that everything around me was a mechanism of sorts; for instance, when I looked at an object or machine I would imagine how they function and operate layer by layer. Everyday disciplining and drilling my mind to force a thought process of cold logic and seeing connections—modelling patterns with logical reasoning. It's a state of mind I would use at work, but this time I dived in much deeper.

Admittedly, it's a kind of strange headspace to enter into—one goes very quiet, one's eyes open wider, emotions are silenced, feelings are ignored, one takes a step back and starts thinking like a machine. Small information starts to collate as data points are mapped together, just like a jigsaw but using data.

On that Sunday (the day before I arrived), the Mike and Steve went to setup and stayed the night. **Whatever** the source of this activity was - **it didn't disappoint**, as during the night the cameramen pushed upstairs and all strange physical activity started to occur: small cups getting pushed over, marbles banging off the walls like stones... This was the first time either of them had personally witnessed paranormal activity this close and personal - and it seriously shook them up, rushing down the stairs in a panic.

Below: *As the camera does its first sweep the cups were all stacked, as the camera pointed away there was a hard impact sound, on the second sweep the top cup had fallen down. Like a small hard object or projectile was flown through them*

The day came and I set off for 30 East Drive; unfortunately the "Triboelectric field meters" I had ordered had been intercepted by the UK customs and held it for review. This meant the package missed my planned pickup point and delivery. While this was a huge disappointment, I pushed forward thinking "let's see what we get." 30 East Drive did not disappoint.

When I finally arrived I was surprised at the appearance of the house! It was just this old council house on an estate, the interior was old, and beaten (which was kind of creepy in and of itself), but overall it was **nothing special**. I walked in there, met Michael and Steve, who had setup already, and had myself a cup of tea. The place felt fine—no big deal at all.

I jumped online and found a layout plan from http://forgottenparanormal.co.uk/page19.html of the home.

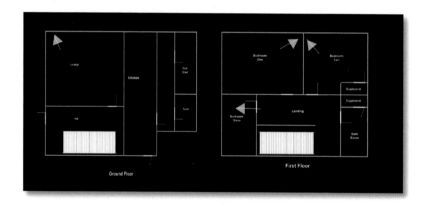

Michael (below) had already set himself up in the kitchen area with microphones wired through the whole house. He told me about the previous night's events. At the time, I just took it at face value; even though they had some amazing video footage, I figured this is the kind of thing one needs to witness for themselves.

And I didn't have to wait long.

The first night will always be one of the most amazing experiences of my life. We were upstairs in bedroom two, lights were off, and we just stood there in silence. I just asked, "Is anyone here?" At that moment, from downstairs we heard a door aggressively bang 8 times and something (soon identified to be two marbles) grazed my face. **For a moment** we just stood there in amazement, and then ran down the stairs to where the banging was happening—it was the coal shed door, this **activity replicated the night before** and had been recorded in real-time on the digital recorders.

Below: door on the left is the internal coal shed, witnessed many times to bang aggressively as If someone hitting it with their hand.

However, by the second day nothing more had was gone on. The events from the previous night hadn't continued and all was silent.

I decided to do my best to provoke whatever was there to get a reaction. I grabbed a camera bracket with fresh 3M tape (professional mounting adhesive) and stuck it on a glass panelled picture—dead top centre located at the top of the stairs. This was a picture with a prayer inscribed, The stairs were said to be very active and I was hoping to record something..

I walked down the stairs, and while the others went outside for a cigarette, I popped to the restroom. As I was sitting there suddenly I heard the walkie talkie upstairs auto audio alert speaking *"low voltage"* and then a **loud bang** at the base of the stairs.

This moment was interesting as not only was it highly unlikely for the bracket to naturally fall off, apparently there was a **sudden power drop** just before **an action occurred** this was strange as the walkie talkies were freshly charged and were relatively new also had been working fine all day - then to top it off, I heard a deep growl from the other side of the door... interestingly I found the event quite amusing as I was sitting there on the toilet halfway through a number two while this growling was coming closer. I thought, *"Well, I'm in the right place I guess..."*

As I left I called the guys over and we all walked over to find the bracket sitting on the bottom of the stairs, and I thought; *"now this is interesting!"*

The 3M tape is so strong that one could hang a bag of sugar from it—there is more chance of the glass breaking than the tape giving away, so this event was totally strange! **This was the behaviour I was looking for! An action that *seemingly* went against physics**... The 3M pad itself wasn't torn therefore wasn't forced, the only way I could think of this occurring is if the chemical bonding had been nullified somehow?

So, I wanted to see if it would **replicate** with less weight each time.

I took the bracket and made it lighter by removing the camera and again applied fresh 3M tape. Again I stuck it dead centre and as I turned around to walk away— it popped off within seconds with the clock suddenly tipping towards me.

Below is the sequence of events as captured on a full spectrum camera.

Below: *The moment below the 3M bracket was reattached to the glass pane, I turned around to walk down the stairs*

Below: *One second later, I heard the pop & instinctively ducked down, and turned around to see what it was*

Below: *As the bracket fell, the clock then tipped forwards towards me, the clock was quite stable and therefore it's very unlikely the bracket would have caused the clock to push forwards.*

Unfazed - I turn and catch the clock falling and reset it to its original position

I remove the protective camera box that held the (already removed camera) At this point it only consisted of the base plate and a small bracket, the glass was cleaned and again **fresh 3M tape** was attached - **again making sure the tape stuck down solid.**

It should be mentioned the weight this type of tape can hold averages around 10 to 15 pounds - (possibly even more these days) but the reality was this camera bracket was less that 2 pounds and **imposed no stress bearing load at all.**

Note: It should be noted that the clock is a main focus of activity with it getting pushed down during the Pritchard periods. The same clock is also documented in the film "When the Lights Went Out." as seen below

*Below is a still image from the 30 East Drive movie, **"when the lights went out"**.*

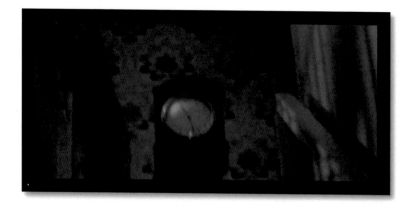

I set the cameras up, and again...

*Within minutes **the event replicated** with the lightweight bracket popping off the glass*

Totally defying the laws of physics

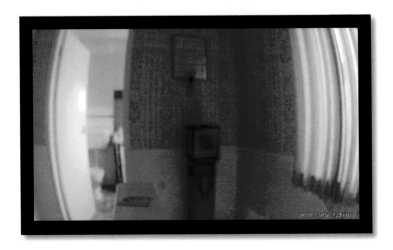

I reset the test again this time with even less weight - and again

It replicates

02/01/2015 12:56:54

The constant in this is the tape - same bonding strength - but What I noticed was the force appeared to have halved every time it occurred, the first one was **strong**, the second was **medium** and the last was **weak**; this tells me that whatever is doing this has **some kind of capacitor** that charges and discharges to perform actions. This by its very nature told me

Whatever was causing this effect had a technical behaviour behind it rather than a human behaviour...

The video recordings observed the **same process** with the tape itself appearing to **suddenly lose it chemical bonding** dropping vertically **with very little if any horizontal force, while a human behaviour** would be someone trying to pull it off **in different ways using direct force.**

I did set this test up again but this time nothing happened, it would seem whatever was performing that action had run out of resource, and was unable to continue.

As the evening pushed on the numbers of the thermometers started to change this also caught my attention—666—widely observed around the paranormal community as is defined as the mark of the beast

Reference: *https://en.wikipedia.org/wiki/Number_of_the_Beast*

- *The number of the beast (Greek: Ἀριθμὸς τοῦ θηρίου, Arithmos tou Thēriou), also known as the devil's number in the Book of Revelation, of the New Testament, is associated with the Beast of Revelation in chapter 13, verse 18. In most manuscripts of the New Testament and in English translations of the Bible, the number of the beast is six hundred and sixty-six or χξς (in Greek numerals, χ represents 600, ξ represents 60 and ς represents 6)*

In the I.T. world, numbers are not just random but are assigned for a reason. In the mathematical world, the number 666 is known as a Triangular number. A triangular number counts the objects that can form an equilateral triangle. As such, "666 is the sum of the first 36 natural numbers (i.e. $1 + 2 + 3 + ... + 34 + 35 + 36 = 666$), and thus it is a triangular number." I found a website that explains it perfectly:

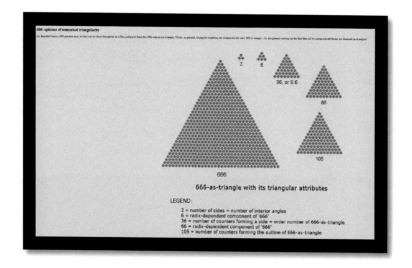

Reference:

http://www.whatabeginning.com/ASPECTS/Triangle666.htm

Reference:

https://link.springer.com/chapter/10.1007/11893295_114

- *Triangular numbers - *fuzzy numbers* are used in Neural networks, Neural networks are the base of advance AI.A fuzzy LMS (least-mean-square algorithm) neural network evaluation model, with fuzzy triangular numbers as inputs, is set up to compare the importance of different indices. The model also has a strong self-learning ability so that calculations are greatly reduced and simplified. Further, decision maker's specific preferences for uncertainty, i.e., risk-averse, risk-loving or risk-neutral, are considered in the evaluation model.*

If this 666 number is appearing in the locations on different electronic mediums then whatever this presence is could be using a form of AI, and an AI number is shown... What the exact significance of that number has yet to be seen

This kind of number is defined as a complex number, a number a machine or system would use... I wondered what if the number 666 was actually **a notification code** which states a system is now **online** or **armed**.

Below - *66.6 Fahrenheit = 19.22 Celsius (C) 30 East Drive temperature*

I spent two sleepless nights of watching strange electronic effects from the walkie talkies strange readings on the K2 meters strange behaviour on my computer with it randomly locking for no reason and strange physical feelings.

Around 2am on my 3rd and final night, all the camera batteries were flat and we were physically and psychologically shattered. We all stood as the bottom of the staircase and I shouted, *"Right here is your last chance! We don't have any cameras—nothing! Come say hello!"*

At this moment I turned my head, and I saw what everyone had been talking about—a vertical black mass -that slowly moved away towards the kitchen area. I didn't say anything at the time as I didn't want the guys to react. As we moved into the lounge area, I spotted this vertical black mass in the kitchen though the curtains watching us. I glared at it and it suddenly moved away; **this was exactly what I needed** to start putting the pieces together.

What I observed was a vertical **black mass** that moved in a digital fashion. The characteristic movements were unique as it did not **speed up** or **slow down**. It moved as a set rate—**stops dead** and changes direction—meaning it moves without friction, resistance, or weight. In other words it moved like a machine.

As we all settled down to sleep, my mind was trying to make sense of the past few days. I felt I had been put in a defensive position, and was out of balance. The fact was—**the source of this activity was interactive and demonstrated some interesting capabilities, such as multiple actions around the house at one time, physical force on objects, strange electronic effects on radios and computers and psychological effects on the group itself.**

What bugged me the most was, people say *"this is a spirit of a dead human"*, but all **the behaviour patterns were all wrong.** Humans in general are pack animals; like the company of others; are information sharing; and co-operative. While **all this presence does** is throw marbles around, cause strange electronic effects on walkie-talkies/computers and bangs on doors and walls. **When one goes upstairs** events happen **downstairs and vice versa**—like a cat and mouse game forcing people to move from one part of the house to another. What came clear was that even though this presence was capable of some amazing tricks **it wasn't hostile** but **its behaviour was subversive, confusing, indirect and avoidant.**

The next day we woke up at 6am exhausted and mentally burned out, I had a ton of footage to work though and my brain was scrambled, I struggled to do even basic tasks, and with that in mind I decided to leave around 2pm.

The Aftermath

Back home in London and all was fine up to the fourth day. Then, around 8.30 pm as I'm lying on my bed, a vertical black mass suddenly rushed passed.

I observe it move up the wall and take a left through the door. Within seconds my wireless router stopped working; I saw this black mass return into my room in which it then faded...

The very next day scratching on the top corners of the walls started—sounded like something with sharp nails. I also observed sudden changes in light—I would sit at my computer at night time and the light would suddenly change as if something darted past.

Over the following days, I observed a black orb the size of an orange flying around my room, finally I switched on all my triboelectric field meters (which had finally arrived) and the previously hard to trigger detectors lit up like a Christmas tree!

I found there was a constant movement of static energy flowing around my room... In the images below, I moved the detectors around and I continued to get constant readings.

At night I heard lots of taps and bangs, sounded like small rubber balls were bouncing off my walls, which all got a bit annoying. The last event was approximately two weeks later; at around 9pm, I was home from work and lying on my bed. Then all of a sudden I observed a small ball of light shoot up from the floor—stop dead as if to look at me. At that moment, I heard the same scratching as before, but this time next to my head **directly on the wall behind me**.

And with that, it shot out through the window, after which all general activity stopped.

But the psychological effects lasted for months...

All along I felt terrible—not ill as in sick **but very mentally distorted**, even my vision seemed to have changed. At night the dark seemed to be denser—I had even seemed to have lost my confidence when walking in darkness as it felt like a **lot of eyes were watching me non-stop**.

From been very chilled out before East drive, post East drive I felt in a **constant state of high aggression** with my body feeling more **like a machine than a living thing**. For the first time in years I suffered from **stress related tension** in my throat, it was like I was getting strangled. I felt **electronically burnt out**, like my **nervous system had been fried** and was struggling to transmit signals... I wondered what could be causing this. I found that many paranormal investigators have experienced exactly the same effects and it's **commonly known as the paranormal hangover**.

Some of my closest friends who noticed a change in my behaviour asked me what happened. Strangely, I found it hard to explain. It was like there was a mental block preventing me from thinking, it kind of felt like I had bitten off more than I could chew and my mind was struggling to process it.

Finally a few months' later things settled down and I felt a lot better, I got in touch with the camera guys. To my amazement they had also been experiencing strange effects, with objects explosively shattering for no reason and also hearing a disembodied deep scratchy voice at night.

It took a year before I started reviewing some of the footage in my flat. I began to send a few people some strange bits; I did this by grabbing my phone and filming the silent video straight off the screen. To my surprise on playback I heard an EVP as video was playing...

KEEP OUT—I told you, I'm here to touch!

I had showed a few people this recording and it freaked them out! They asked how I could sleep at night, but the truth is the more it spoke and the more actions it performed, the quicker one can find certain traits. After all, to figure out the trick—you need to keep replaying it...

Over time, minor bits of activity would still occur but it no longer fazed me, you would have thought this was intimidating but it became kind of amusing. One night I was laying on my bed and something hissed directly in my right ear, I didn't react, I just said, **"Is that the best you can do?"**

Finally over time, everything cooled down. The day came when I got my head got back on straight and I could approach this experience with a clear mind... I felt quite happy that I went, I saw, and I witnessed activity all first-hand. I successfully emerged out the other side a little battered and bruised but richer for the experience. Now it was time to put on my I.T. hat and treat it like any normal reverse engineering project.

PART EIGHT

IMAGE AND BEHAVIOUR ANALYSIS
OF OBSERVED PHENOMENON

As mentioned, I saw what's called **"the black monk" up close and personal.** I started to observe its actions and behaviour. The following descriptions are technical in nature so please bear with me.

What I observed is a vertical **black mass** that moves around the house in a digital fashion, its characteristic movements are unique as it does not **speed up** or **slow down.** It moves as a set rate—**stops dead** and changes direction—meaning it moves without friction or resistance or weight.

After my visit, I had my cameraman, Michael, take one of the Triboelectric field meters to try it out. One evening he managed to get access into East drive again. He found that whatever is in the building was emitting **strong vertical static fields** which could be tracked as this presence passed over.

I managed to get hold of a **full spectrum image** of this **black mass, which matched my observation**, and loaded it into an **image processing program.** Observe the images below taken moments apart, one that is clear and one with this black mass effect at the top of the stairs.

Reference*: Bil Bungay*

On filtering, I can extract more visual data and I noticed some-thing, though the noise.

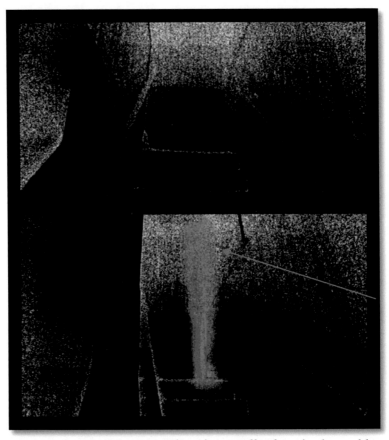

Bottom image: Top centre, there is a small sphere is observable within the distortion, that seemed to be emitting a vertical field of some kind.

Though contacts within the community I managed to source more images that matched my observation, again they see a black vertical mass moving without friction or sound.

Reference: Bil Bungay

And again, with a little contrast increase - notice this sphere becomes visible

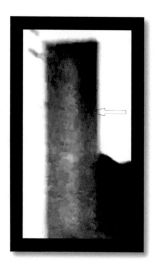

Below: Image inverted for detail, and this sphere becomes even clearer.

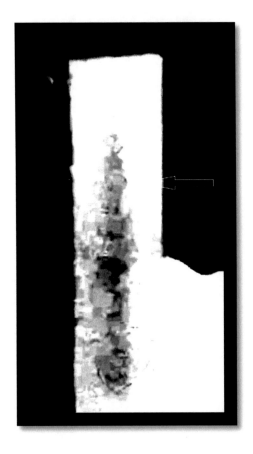

So what could be occurring though the noise?

Black mass/

Masking technique

With solid sphere in the upper centre

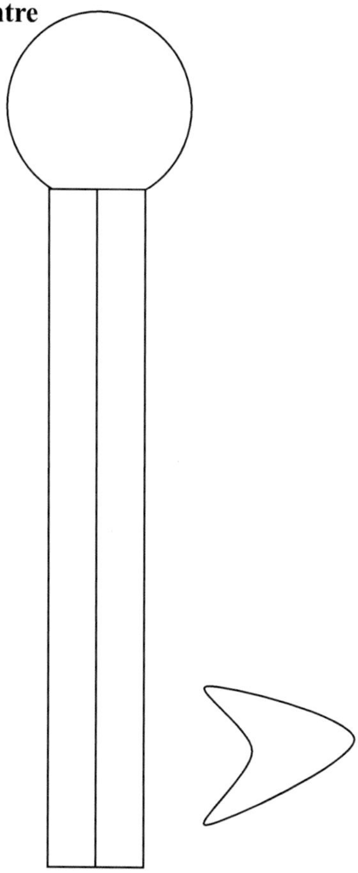

Vertical line of force,

With by-product to the right

If you look back at the previous image and follow the vertical line of force you will observe that at dead centre of the noise is the outline of a small sphere.

- This sphere appears to be **emitting a field** which is creating the light distortion

When in close proximity, this **presence** has been observed to trigger both electromagnetic field detectors (EMF) and vertical Static field detectors. The question begs, could an **electronic – field based propulsion system** emit both of these field types?

The answer it **very likely**, with high voltage fields and static emitted as by-products.

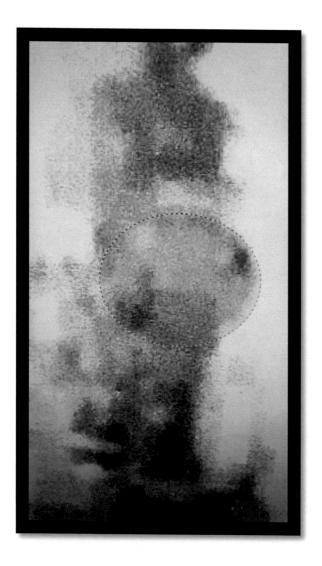

A few weeks later, I got hold of these images taken from inside East drive. These are the most telling—could this be the same object as above without the black mass **masking** effect? By observation this silver sphere size is approximate to that of a cricket ball, and matches the approximate size of the sphere outlined in the black mass image **figure #**

What is observable is a small silver ball with light reflecting off its surface.

- Close up, one observes **light** distortions surrounding the silver sphere.
- This would indicate that this physical object is emitting a field that is capable of bending/absorbing light/blocking light.
- This object has also been photographed& filmed in a **transparent state**—in this state it's observed to have the ability to pass through solid objects. Although the naked, unaided human eye can't see it, close up these objects are reflective to IR, this **could be defined** as a **Quantum state.** The best way to describe this state is that of a grey area between **one reality and other**, converting from a solid object to the appearance of a solid bubble that can pass through solid barriers such as walls.

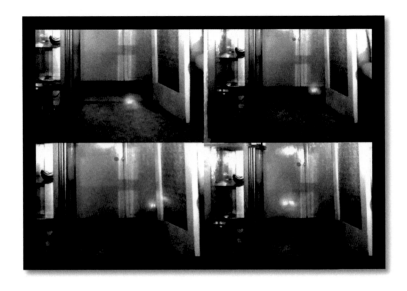

Reference: Bil Bungay

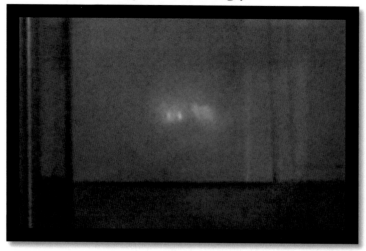

- These small spheres are known to be one of the most common UFO types observed around the world.

I looked into Military records; to my surprise I found records of reports from WW2 that matched the appearance and capabilities of this object.

The US Air Force called them "Foo-Fighters"— small silver spheres that would suddenly appear in front of aircraft, reported to track the aircraft for miles while flying just above the wing tips in perfect synchronicity.

With no wings or flight control surfaces, this would indicate a **propulsion** and **flight** system that is very advanced and utilising **electronic field based propulsion.**

- This object would not be **spiritual,** but **artificial in nature** utilizing an advanced technology.
- Exactly the same flight **characteristics** have been observed by

what the paranormal community refer to as **Spirit Orbs.**

- **The question is, "*have these objects been misidentified?*" "*And if so, why are they operating inside buildings?***

Separate from my own research, I found a presentation from Richard Greer from 2017 who is the Founder of the US Disclosure Project.

Reference: *https://www.youtube.com/watch?v=h-GWw1HscuYandfeature=youtu.be*

Greer states, *"There were these things called foo-fighters, yes it's a rock group and Dave Grohi great guy—he named his band after what I'm about to tell you, a foo-fighter aside from been a fun rock band were objects flying around our aircraft in world war two. Sometimes they were fully materialized—Hard—Most of the time they were an energy field that that looked spherical and they could come through an aircraft even coming down the centre of an aircraft and out the other end. This became a huge concern for the Allies and the US President on behalf of the Allies dispatched a man called General Jimmy Doolittle to the theatres of operations in Europe to find out what these things were, these objects would disrupt electromagnetic signals they would have effects on the gravity around the aircraft including effects on the guidance systems compasses etc, so we thought it was a secret Nazi weapon and we found out though our spies that the Germans thought it was a secret Allied weapon. So General Dolittle investigated this and came back to the White House and reported back to President Roosevelt and said 'Sir, these are interplanetary vehicles.' "*

As mentioned above, this object can enter a quantum state **and pass though solid objects**, and also present themselves as **bright spheres** with **an energy field around them.**

Could these silver sphere objects seen in East drive and other active locations be modern day foo-fighters?

Side-by-side comparison

Reference: *Bil Bungay*

Above: Reported Ghost Orb at East drive observed as transaparent and able to pass through solid objects.

"Sometimes they were fully materialized—Hard—Most of the time they were an energy field that that looked spherical and they could come through an aircraft even coming down the centre of an aircraft and out the other end."

Richard Greer

The common-reported Spirit Orb is displayed in the image below. Taken in a graveyard with an IR camera, are we actually observing a metalic sphere with an ironised electrical fields surrounding it?

Below: *The common reported **Silver Sphere** drone type UFO in daytime taken in Cheesefoot Head, Wiltshire UK.*

Reference: *https://www.colinandrews.net/Orb-UFO-BEAMS-CheesefootHead.html*

Below: *East Drive ghost Orb image enhanced*

Reference: *Bil Bungay*

One of these small silver spheres even made the newspapers, such as this image taken during a hiking holiday in Albania. Ljuboten or Luboten (in Albanian) is a peak of the Šar Mountains located on the border between Kosovo[a] and North Macedonia. Its elevation is 2,498 m (8,196 ft). Ljuboten, although not the highest peak of the range, is somewhat isolated from the rest of the mountains, making it visible from both Pristina and Skopje.

PICTURED: Is bizarre hovering metallic ball a drone sent by UFO?

EXCLUSIVE: PARANORMAL investigators are looking into this bizarre picture which appears to show a metallic ball hovering behind a group of hikers.

By JON AUSTIN
PUBLISHED: 13:29, Thu, Nov 3, 2016 | UPDATED: 13:45, Thu, Nov 3, 2016

SHARE f TWEET in P

0

The UFO orb can be seen the left of the man on the furthest left of the image

Conclusion

As these objects are highly unusual in abilities and behaviour **they could be defined as a missing link** Mainstream paranormal researchers have somehow avoided; this oversight could be explained as the desire to have an earthly relatable explanation, as it always feels more acceptable than something *other*. The reality is…

On observation of these spheres they share approximately:

- **Same size**
- **Physical appearance**
- **Flight characteristics**
- **Same ability to fly though solid objects**
- **Both utilising a field based propulsion system**
- **Both capable of unusual electronic effects**

Due to the unusual technical capabilities, the chance of this connection being a coincidence is **extremely unlikely.**

The same strange electronic and physical effects were observed by WW2 aircrews as are observed by current haunted houses and high activity areas. Therefore it's logical to assume all these images are of the **same object type** operating in different **states and modes configured to do a specific task.**

Question: *"If these are physical objects then where could they be deployed from?"*

An interesting video filmed by Pedro Hernandez in Mexico City - May 22 2009 may give some answers; where an strange object in the sky was deploying hundreds of smaller drone-type objects—see screen shots below.

Reference: https://www.youtube.com/watch?v=9jKN5pGY174

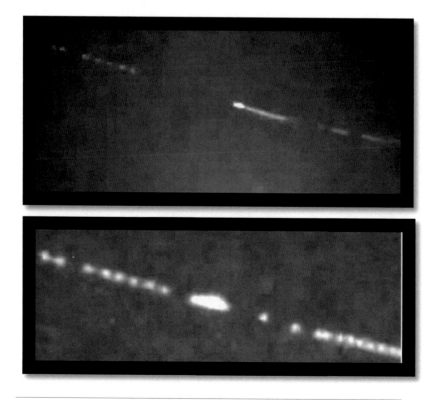

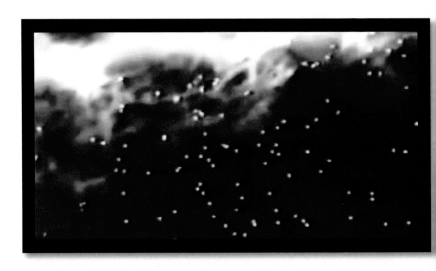

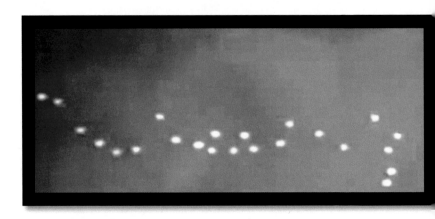

The reality is all deployments, be that I.T based or Space based requires a custom developed process to perform "that" deployment task, and this process is generally set in stone, or has very controlled change mechanism. This means the same deployment process should be replicated around world. The following is the observed process.

First: A Single airborne object will tip to the" left" releasing **three spheres**, once deployed these spheres appear to network with each other, taking the configuration of a rotating triangle, this could be performing a 360 degree narrow band radar sweep before deployment as described below.

Images below are still from a video Jim Martin – CE5 Producer

Below my analysis of what appears to be occuring

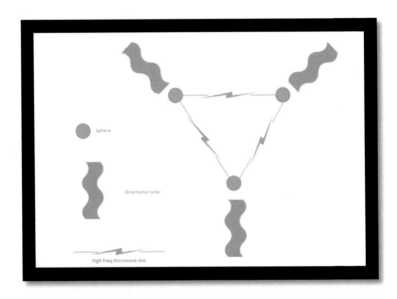

Second: This stage is "deployment" where the object tilts to the "right" and deploys a batch of approx 50 to 100 spheres - depending on the design of the craft dictates the ejection process; the deployed spheres appear to be only visible under IR and not directly visible to human sight. Same is observed in haunted buildings where spheres are seen passing though walls and flying around the rooms.

PART NINE

MILITARY HISTORY OF OBSERVED PHENOMENON

Reference: http://www.project1947.com/fig/1945a.htm

PROJECT 1947

UFO REPORTS - 1945

The following is military and media reports of these silver sphere objects

St. Louis, Missouri, <u>POST DISPATCH</u> - 2 January, 1945

Mysterious 'Foo Fighters,' Balls Of Fire, Trail U.S. Night Flyers

Thought at First to Be Explosive, but None as Yet Has Damaged a Plane

A UNITED STATES NIGHT FIGHTER BASE, France, Jan. 2 (AP)– American fighter pilots engaged in night missions over Germany report the Nazis have come up with a new "secret weapon" - mysterious balls of fire which race along beside their planes for miles. Yank pilots have dubbed them "foo fighters," and at first thought they might explode, but so far there is no indication that any planes have been damaged by them. Some pilots have expressed belief that the "foo fighter" was designed strictly as a psychological weapon.

Intelligence reports seem to indicate that it is radio-controlled and can keep pace with planes flying 300 miles an hour. Lt. Donald Meiers of Chicago, said there are three types of "foo fighters"

- *red balls of fire that fly along at wing tip;*
- *a vertical row of three balls of fire which fly in front of the planes, and a group of about 15 lights which appear off in the distance*

The pilots of this Beaufighter squadron—in operation since September, 1943—find these fiery balls the weirdest thing they have as yet encountered. "A 'foo fighter' picked me up recently at 700 feet and chased me 20 miles down the Rhine Valley," Meiers said. "I turned to starboard and two balls of fire turned with me. I turned to the port side and they turned with me. We were going 260 miles an hour and the balls were keeping right up with us." "On another occasion when a 'Foo-Fighter' picked us up, I dived at 360 miles an hour. It kept right off our wing tips for awhile and then zoomed into the sky." "When I first saw the things, I had the horrible thought that a German on the ground was ready to press a button and explode them. But they didn't explode or attack us. They just seem to follow us like will-o-the-wisps."

*Lt. Wallace Gould of Silver Creek, N. Y., **said the lights followed his wing tips** for a while and then, in a few seconds, zoomed 20,000 feet into the air and out of sight.*

TIME Magazine - 15 January, 1945

Foo-Fighter

If it was not a hoax or an optical illusion, it was certainly the most puzzling secret weapon that Allied fighters have yet encountered. Last week U.S. night fighter pilots based in France told a strange story of balls of fire which for more than a month have been follow-

ing their planes at night over Germany. No one seemed to know what, if anything, the fireballs were supposed to accomplish. Pilots, guessing it was a new psychological weapon, named it the "foo-fighter."

Their descriptions of the apparition varied, but they agree that the mysterious flares stuck close to their planes and appeared to follow them at high speed for miles. One pilot said that a foo-fighter, appearing as red balls off his wing tips, stuck with him until he dove at 360 miles an hour; then the balls zoomed up into the sky.

Sceptical scientists, baffled by the whole affair, were inclined to dismiss the fireballs as an illusion, perhaps an afterimage of light which remained in the pilots's eyes after they had been dazzled by flak bursts. But front-line correspondents and armchair experts had a Buck Rogers field day.

They solemnly guessed:

1) *That the balls of fire were radio-controlled (an obvious absurdity, since they could not be synchronized with a plane's movements by remote control);*
2) *That they were created by "electrical induction of some sort";*
3) *That they were attracted to a plane by magnetism.*

The correspondents further guessed that foo-fighters were intended:

1) *To dazzle pilots;*
2) *To serve as aiming points for anti-aircraft gunners;*
3) *To interfere with a plane's radar;*
4) *To cut a plane's ignition, thus stop its engine in midair.*

Some scientists suggested another possibility: that the fireballs were nothing more than St. Elmo's fire, a reddish brush-like discharge of atmospheric electricity which has often been seen near the tips of church steeples, ships' masts and yardarms. It often appears at a plane's wing tips.

January 15, 1945

*Last month pilots reported that they had seen **mysterious floating silvery balls**, apparently another "secret weapon" in daylight flight over Germany.*

XII Tactical Air Command Intelligence Information Bulletin

No. 6

"Flak Developments":

There have however been several reports of the phenomenon which is described as "silver balls", *seen mainly below 10,000 feet; tentative suggestions have been made as to their origin and purpose, but as **yet no satisfactory explanation has been found**. The bulletin for June 4, 1945, discusses reports from Japan: Mention has previously been made in these pages to the existence of German airborne controlled missiles Hs.298, Hs.293, X4 and Hs.117. Many reports have been received from Bomber Command crews of flaming missiles being directed at, and sometimes following the aircraft, suggesting the use of remote control and/or homing devices. It is known that the Germans kept their Japanese Allies informed of technical developments and the following report, taken verbatim from Headquarters, U. S. A. F. P. O. A. G.2 Periodic Report No. 67, further suggests that the Japanese are using similar weapons to those reported by our own crews:*

"During the course of a raid by Super-Fortresses on the Tachikawa aircraft plant, and the industrial area of Kawasaki, both in the Tokyo area, a number of Super-Fortresses reported having been followed or pursued by "red balls of fire" described as being ap-

*proximately **the size of a basketball** with a phosphorescent glow. Some were reported to have tails of blinking light. These "balls" appeared generally out of nowhere, only one having been seen to ascend from a relatively low altitude to the rear of a B-29. No accurate estimate could be reached as to the distance between the balls and the B-29's. No amount of evasion of the most violent nature succeeded in shaking the balls. They succeeded in following the Super-Fortresses through rapid changes of altitude and speed and sharp turns, and held B-29s' courses through clouds. One B-29 reported outdistancing a ball only by accelerating to 295 mph, after which the pursuing ball turned around and headed back to land. Individual pursuits lasted as long as six minutes, and one ball followed a Super-Fortress 30 miles out to sea. The origin of the balls is not known. Indication points to some form of radio-direction, either from the ground or following enemy aircraft. The apparent objective of the balls, no doubt, is destruction of the Super-Fortresses by contact. **Both interception and AA [anti-aircraft] have proved entirely ineffective;** the enemy has apparently developed a new weapon with which to attempt countering our thrusts."*

Reference:

http://foofighters.greyfalcon.us/photos.html?fbclid=IwAR0AAt8sC8 o8AQrOMA5iCCKYiwC_uz8KxH2nxIx3qV3a5oWblX8-eYtbV5U

Below: *is a public domain image collection of these foo-fighter objects*

A Japanese Sally bomber (some say it's a Betty), with a UFO (Foo Fighter) trailing it.

Italy, 1945

Observations

During this War period of time, this strange airborne sphere activity was **unwelcome** and was terrifying for the aircrews. Their planes started acting unpredictably over the sea or near what was enemy airspace, with conventional airborne ballistic weapons having zero effect on them. Notice the solid light; this is very likely to be the by-product of a high voltage artificial field based propulsion system which ionizes the air causing an electrical gas interaction resulting in photons/light—a common trait among UFO sightings.

What replicates here is the reported ability to pass though solid objects. On occasion, aircrews witnessed these objects pass though the aircraft's wings without causing damage. Likewise, much to the frustration of the AA gunners, bullets had zero effect. **The spheres also demonstrated an array of strange electronic effect**s on the planes instruments, in some cases stalling the engine, altering control of the aircraft, and even affecting the gravity around the airframe itself. This demonstrates that advanced electronic and gravitational countermeasures are in-place and in effect whether intentional or not **demonstrates a weaponized capability** within these spheres. As the images demonstrate, these spheres appear to **be currently operating in buildings.** If that is indeed the case, **is it really a surprise that people are experiencing** the same strange electronic and gravitational effects observed in active locations with radios playing up, batteries losing power, and computers failing etc. By using its field based propulsion system it can artificially create force on objects, creating movement and impact, and then causing doors/walls to bang/and objects to be thrown around at will. Thus, it is perceived as paranormal activity. When we think about it, if one was to take a magnet to the 12th century and demonstrated its abilities in public—you could probably count the seconds before someone calls out—witch! With that, the mob ensues... what was perceived as black magic back then is now perceived as paranormal.

The only difference is the technology (as mentioned later in the book) and construction of these spheres is by far beyond magnets, far beyond our **current energy technologies**, and **far beyond our nuclear material capability.** Therefore its actions and capabilities are understandably **perceived as magical or supernatural.**

The scientific world's current research is only scratching the surface of quantum mechanics. Scientists have theories on how **this pass though of physical objects is possible**; as far as I can tell the closest current explanation is an effect called **Quantum Tunnelling.** Quantum tunnelling is the quantum mechanical phenomenon where a subatomic particle passes through a potential barrier that it cannot surmount under the provision of classical mechanics.

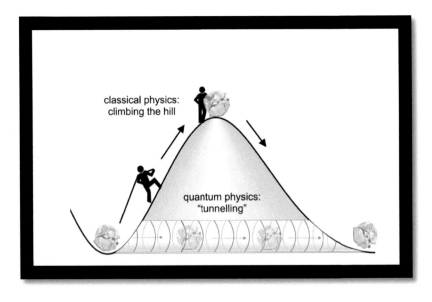

classical physics:
climbing the hill

quantum physics:
"tunnelling"

Above: *A diagram demonstrating the ball analogy of quantum tunnelling to climb the hill a ball would need sufficient energy, but with quantum tunnelling there's a chance that the ball could randomly "tunnel" through the hill and appear on the other side*

Reference: *Image Max Planck Institute for Quantum Optics.*

***Quantum tunnelling* or *tunneling* (US) *is the* quantum** *mechanical phenomenon where a subatomic particles probability disappears from one side of a potential barrier and appears on the other side without any probability current (flow) appearing inside the well.*

Reference: *https://en.wikipedia.org/wiki/Quantum_tunnelling*

As I mentioned at 30 East drive...

I, as many have, observed a vertical **black mass** that, "moves around the house in a digital fashion, its movement characteristic are unique as it does not **speed up** or **slow down** it moves as a set rate—**stops dead** and changes direction—meaning it moves without friction or resistance or weight. It's also been observed that this **black mass** can pass though solid objects such as walls." these are both examples of advanced field based propulsion and advanced quantum tunnelling capabilities, **and finally the images of the small silver sphere object hovering just inches from the floor.**

It's logical to state...

The flight characteristics and its physical description both match that of sphere-type UFO / WW2 Foo-Fighter objects. It would appear these same objects that were playing havoc with the Air force back in 1945, are now operating in buildings. **Operating on a low-to-ground basis,** they use **physical countermeasures** to hide in **low light environments,** creating a **black mass effect around the sphere.** This masking blocks photons, creating an **adaptive camouflage** allowing these objects to be in close proximity **without visual detection.**

An example of this camouflage technique can be provided by the defence contractors BAE SYSTEMS—same idea but achieved by masking the thermal signature for night operations.

Reference: https://www.youtube.com/watch?v=wlLqdFsMnCE

Images below show the ADAPTIV, an adaptive thermal signature management developed by BAE Systems in Sweden. The video clips show a recent test, demonstrating how the 'invisibility cloak' on the CV90 light tank turns the vehicle invisible, by blending into its surroundings. **Like all advanced technology it can be perceived as magic.**

'ADAPTIV' Blends the vehicle into the background

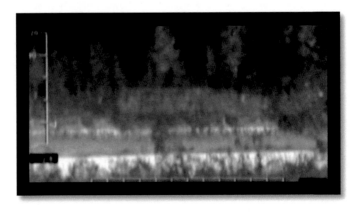

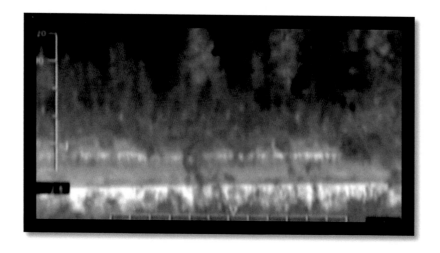

Question: *If these object mostly operate in a semi-transparent quantum state... Could the paranormal community be misidentifying these objects as Spirit orbs? If so, what would they look like?*

In this quantum state, these objects appear as near transparent. Like a glass sphere in water, the sphere-like UFOs sometimes become visible and other times not. Most of the time people spot these objects not with natural eyesight but on **camera**; this is because cameras (and animals) have greater sensitivity to the ultraviolent spectrum.

Let's look how these objects emit light...

Think about the chemical makeup of the open-air. The spheres **field-based propulsion system**—when operating under a **constant high voltage state**—would cause the same effect as **natural lighting**. So the question is, how does **natural** lighting emit light?

By volume open, dry air contains 78.09% **nitrogen**, 20.95% **oxygen**, 0.93% **argon**, 0.04% **carbon dioxide**, and small amounts of other gases. Air also contains a variable amount of **water vapour**, on average around 1% at sea level, and 0.4% over the entire atmosphere.

Under **high energy**, a natural electrical gas interaction occurs which **emits photons.**

Oxygen **emits** either a greenish-yellow **light** (the most familiar **colour** of the aurora) or a red **light,** while **nitrogen** generally gives off a blue **light**. The oxygen and **nitrogen** molecules also **emit ultraviolet light** (hence why these objects are spotted on cameras but we can't see them at the time).

However, the overall colour is very dependent on the **environmental factors at the time.** Natural lighting can emit a **range of colours** from white, red, yellow, green, blue, pink, purple, violet, cyan, and even to orange depending upon the presence of water vapour, dust, pollution, rain, or hail.

People observe these Spirit orbs as a range of colours as well; logically this could simply be the result of the above, same electronic gas effects operating in different environments.

According to
https://paranormal.lovetoknow.com/Ghost_Orbs_Different_Colors

The researchers explain the **mainstream paranormal perception** of what the **different colours mean**, and I have added my inserts on each description below.

Clear Orbs

Clear orbs may be a sign an entity is trying to communicate with you. The spirit may be trying to let the living know that some kind of significant event happened in that location and that the spirit wants help to move on.

The silver sphere operating in a quantum state visually look

like a moving bubble that seems to flex or distort—sometimes emitting high levels of light other times operating in a low power state.

- **White or Silver Orbs**

Spiritually, white or silver is associated with spirituality and connection with a higher source. Some investigators believe orbs that are either white or silver in appearance are an indication that a spirit is trapped on this plane. It may also be a sign the spirit is there to offer protection to the people in the area. White energy is typically perceived as highly positive in nature.

Spheres operating in a normal state = small silver ball, The blue discharge is the colour of natural lighting travelling through open air, again due to environmental factors

- **Black or Brown Orbs**

Spiritually, many feel black or brown colours are associated with lower spiritual vibrations or heavy energy. Some people interpret this as evil although it isn't necessarily the case. When black or brown orbs appear, some investigators interpret them as a sign the area may be unsafe or negative in nature. Examine such a place with caution, and if you feel uncomfortable or unsafe, leave.

Spheres operating in what could be described as a stealth mode, seen as a small solid black non reflective sphere, in effect the sphere blocks photons (light) from reflecting from the surface, resulting in a super black appearance.

- **Red or Orange Orbs**

From a spiritual perspective, red and orange colours are associated with safety and security, as well as a sense of belonging. While these warm colours are often associated with strong emotions, such as anger and passion, this may not be the case when it comes to ghost orbs. Some paranormal investigators believe a red or orange orb is a sign that an entity has assumed the role of a protector. This could be someone who was charged in life to keep watch or be a caretaker.

Red is Oxygen / Orange is Phosphorus gas

- **Green Orbs**

In spiritual practice, green is associated with the heart. It is also associated with nature. Green orbs are sometimes thought to be an indication of the presence of a human spirit as opposed to one that was never on Earth in human form. Likewise, green orbs may represent love or oneness with nature.

Green is Chlorine gas

- **Blue Orb Meanings**

Blue is spiritually associated with psychic energy and truth. It is a very calming colour, and many people associate it with spiritual guidance. Some people feel blue orbs are a sign of a calming presence or energy while others feel they indicate the presence of a spirit guide in that location.

Blue is Nitrogen

- *Pink Orbs*

Pink is a variable / combination of low amounts of gases

It is a common belief that pink orbs are messengers of love. This can be universal love, such as the spiritual love of an ascended master, guide, teacher or archangel. It can also be a more specific love, such as the love of a deceased family member who takes on the mantle of a spirit orb to say they are still with you. Whoever the messenger is, a pink orb brings the message of encouragement, hope, peace and, always, love

The bottom line is that light **is emitted by the surrounding gas** when an electric current is flowing through it. This **light** by-product results from collisions between atoms within the gas and electrons of the current. As the electrical power is a **constant** (unlike ball lighting)—in its normal state **one would observe a small sphere of solid light passing by in silence**, or in a quantum state one would observe the UV by-product of the propulsion field which will flex and blur with movement.

"Any sufficiently advanced technology is indistinguishable from magic"

Arthur C Clarke

Question: if these are a machine of some sort, have any crashed or gone wrong?

The answer to this, would you believe, is... well it seems they have!

PART TEN

THE BETZ MYSTERY SPHERE

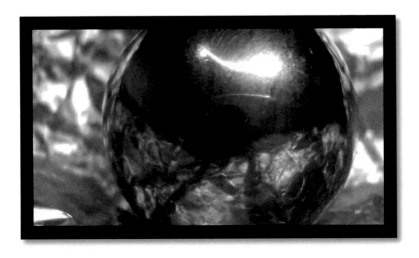

Reference: *https://www.youtube.com/watch?v=w8vgr_oswms*

This is the case of a man finding a silver sphere in the woods after a fire. He brought it home to put on the mantelpiece as an interesting ordainment to look at. Just after a short while, the house started to experience poltergeist activity. This activity scared the family pets and made life very uncomfortable. Logically, the physical appearance matches that of the object in 30 East Drive—and by all accounts it's broken/gone offline.

Reference: *https://intriguedmind.com/whatever-happened-to-the-betz-mystery-sphere/*

A renowned astronomer and ufologist, requested the Betz family send the sphere to him at his office at the Northwestern University in Chicago. The Betz family refused, which was smart on their part. They family retained the ball in their possession, until some inexplicable events changed everything.

The family stated that they started to hear strange organ-like music in the dead of night, **doors began slamming at all hours of the day and night.** So to get to the bottom of the mystery –they contacted the US Navy. They finally let the sphere out of their hands and into the hands of the scientists at the Jacksonville Naval Air Station, with instructions to have a comprehensive report in 2 weeks and if it wasn't identified as "government property", then it should be returned to them.

The metallurgists couldn't get an x-ray of the sphere –they couldn't penetrate the orb! Eventually, they determined the ball was 7.96 inches in diameter and weighed 21.34 pounds. The "shell" of the ball was 1/2 inch thick. And the sphere was made of stainless steel, specifically magnetic ferrous allow #431. "This alloy was magnetic and designed for heat treatment to the highest mechanical properties and corrosion resistance." The Navy also discovered 2 round objects inside the sphere –using a more powerful x-ray, which were surrounded by a halo made of material that had an unusual density. The sphere also had four magnetic poles, two positive and two negative. It had no signs of radioactivity and showed no signs of being an explosive. The Navy returned the sphere to the Betz family.

Dr. Carl Wilson of the Omega Minus One Institute, located in Baton Rouge, Louisiana went to the family home and examined the sphere for over 6 hours. Wilson was quoted in the newspaper stating "Radio waves coming from it and a magnetic field around it" was what he discovered in his examination of the sphere. He confirmed the Navy's discovery of 4 poles and as "the flux capacity of the field appeared to fluctuate in potency based on as a yet uniden-

tified pattern, defied the known laws of physics." He also claimed the "shell" of the orb wasn't stainless steel, but some unknown element.

The Betz family decided to send the sphere to an event held by the National Enquirer, in hopes that maybe the sphere was evidence of an extra-terrestrial probe and could win the $50,000 prize for proof of such from the National Enquirer. Terry was the carrier of the orb. The sphere became the center of attention at the event and another round of tests were conducted on the sphere on April 20 and 21, 1974. Dr. Hynek believed the object was manmade. The Betz family didn't win the prize.

But another scientist colleague of Hynek's investigated the sphere while at the event. Dr. James Albert Harder, from the University of California at Berkley, was intrigued by the sphere. He announced his findings of the sphere at the International UFO Congress in Chicago on June 24, 1977. He concluded (paraphrased) "that due to the internal components, which he believed were made of elements heavier than anything known to science, and claimed the atomic number was higher than 140—it was basically an atomic bomb." And if one drilled into the sphere to get to the internal contents –that it might set it off or offend its extra-terrestrial creators."

Ask yourself—is the 30 East drive object a smaller (possibly more advanced) version of the Betz sphere? **Logically, it could well be...** But like its older version contained the **same coding and behaviours**.

Let's compare images:

Below 30 East Drive Sphere Current day

Below the Betz Sphere 1974

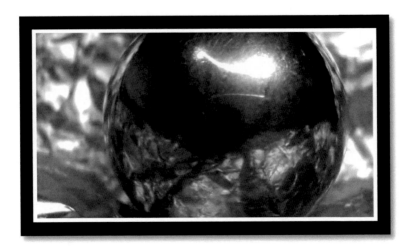

On May 29th 2015, at around 4:00 am, a rabbi in Southeast Ukraine discovered this unexplained sphere of light on the CCTV camera in his synagogue. It is approximately the size of a football/soccer ball and hovered for about 20 seconds before disappearing. This image mirrors the sightings from World War 2 aircrews.

Could this be the same object observed by WW2 aircrews, the same silver sphere but operating in a high energy state?

Could this be the same object operating low level? Notice how it's not a perfect sphere; this is because we are observing the ionized field of gas around it, as it moves the emitted light will distort its surroundings.

In 2013, a CCTV cam in Russia caught a white orb, with obvious signs of intelligence, traveling up and down a secluded road in the woods. Its flight behaviour indicates the white orb is using a form of ground hugging radar as its height alters with the road level.

Betz Sphere 2.0 found in North Texas: Is this the same object as the above images, but it is also offline/broken?

PART ELEVEN

PATTERN ANALYSIS OF OBSERVED PHENOMENON

With all behaviours, be it in nature or within the human domain, there are reoccurring patterns. In the **human** domain people generally **get up, head to work** and **head home** or (now and again) **head out. But we also have an online pattern and behaviour that can be data mined down to a tee, allowing 3rd party companies to know what kind of personality we have, what we like, and what political stance we hold. All of this and more is accomplished just by observing the behaviour patterns of a person; companies can automatically profile billions of users. By the same logic, the secrets of the paranormal can be unlocked by data mining its patterns. So where do we start?**

If one was observed to visit a location five days a week for 8 hours a day, it would be logical to say that one desires a **resource** or service from this location, or that I am employed to perform a task at that that location. In other words, I would head there for a reason and a very good one. After all I wouldn't go there every day purely by coincidence. Observations of my daily pattern would give very clear clues on what I am doing and why. When it comes to the paranormal, the question is—do these patterns exist? And if they do, what could it tell us?

I got in touch with the paranormal community and asked them to provide a list of all of the most haunted areas they could think of. I also included all the well-known areas from internet searches. In total I found 79 confirmed active areas in Great Britain; this number surprised me as I thought it would be much higher. Instead what I found was a small number of what I call restrictive zones, as in locations **so active** that people either can't or struggle to live within them full-time.

This was the key difference between the locations I collected and what I call "white noise." locations where—yes, it might be a little bit active at times—but overall everything was fine. The question is why these restrictive zones are so bad and is there a pattern? And what could be the reason?

Again the numbers struck me as interesting as of 2017, According to the Office of National Statistics

- Source
  https://www.ons.gov.uk/peoplepopulationandcommunity/births deathsandmarriages/deaths
- In 2017 alone there were 533,253 deaths registered in England and Wales which is 4437.75 a month 1110 (rounded up) per week or 159 (rounded up) per day and YET we only have 79 extremely active locations in the whole country thus demonstrating that even in a small country there is a huge discrepancy between human death rates and major paranormal activity, but for arguments sake even if we double that number to 150 - Still we have a huge discrepancy.

I took theses extremely active locations and put them into **Google Earth**—this allowed me to get the **co-ordinances** of each site. From there, I imported the data into Microsoft Excel and then into Microsoft SQL Server for Geospatial analysis.

Geospatial analysis is the gathering, display, and manipulation of imagery, GPS, satellite photography and historical data, described explicitly in terms of geographic coordinates or implicitly, in terms of a street address, postal code, or forest stand identifier as they are applied to geographic models.

Reference: https://ieeexplore.ieee.org/document/5685200

With the Google earth dataset which contains the names and **coordinances**, I then exported that data into Microsoft Excel to format... Once formatted correctly I could then import the data into the SQL Database for geospatial analysis.

The list below is the location dataset:

- 30 east drive, Pontefract
- 39 de grey street hull
- 50 berkley square london
- Athelhampton House - Athelhampton House,Athelhampton,Dorchester
- Barcaldine Castle, Benderloch, Oban
- Beeston (Nottinghamshire) - Crown Inn
- Belgrave Hall - Church Rd, Leicester
- Berry Pomeroy Castle - A381, Berry Pomeroy, Totnes,Devon
- Black boy inn caernafon - Stryd Pedwar a Chwech, Caernarfon
- Bolling Hall, Bradford
- Borley Rectory, Borley, Essex, England
- Bradgate park- leicestershire
- Brislington - City of Bristol
- Buckfastleigh church devon
- Buckland Abbey- Yelverton
- Cannock chase
- Cark (Cumbria)
- Chenies Manor House - Chenies, Rickmansworth WD3 6ER
- Chequers Inn. 51 London Road West- Amersham
- Chillingham Castle - Northumberland

- Chingle hall - Whittingham, Preston, England
- Cock Lane - Smithfield in the City of London
- Croxteth Hall- Liverpool
- Edge Hill - Warwickshire
- Edinburgh Vaults, South Bridge, Edinburgh EH1 1QR
- Ettington Park - Stratford-upon-Avon
- Golden lion hotel, Market Hill, Market Lane, Saint Ives
- Hack Green Secret Nuclear Bunker - French Ln, Nantwich
- Hampton Court Palace, Molesey, East Molesey
- Hever Castle - Hever Rd, Hever, Edenbridge
- Jamaica inn cornwall
- Kingsley - Barnack, Stamford, Peterborough
- Landbeach - Cambridge
- Liangelynnin church- Conwy
- Llancaiach Fawr, Trelewis, Nelson
- Madingley hall - High St, Madingley, Cambridge
- Mary kings close,High Street, 2 Warriston's Close, Edinburgh EH1 1PG
- Minsden Chapel, Langley, Hitchin
- Minster Tavern, Ely Camb
- Morecambe winter garden -209 Marine Rd Central, Morecambe
- Newsham park orphanage liverpool
- Nottingham galleries of justice - (aka Shire Hall) in Nottingham, England
- Nunnington Hall, Nunnington, North Yorkshire, York YO62 5UY
- Old Victorian School Stanhope Street-Nottingham
- Ordsall hall manchester
- Pendle Hill - Lancashire
- Peterborough museum - Priestgate, Peterborough PE1 1LF
- Plas Teg - Mold Road,Pontblyddyn,Mold, Flintshire, Mold
- Powderham castle
- RAF Bircham Newton - Bircham Newton, King's Lynn
- Ram inn,8 Potters Pond, Wotton-under-Edge

- Raynham Hall - Norfolk
- Renishaw Hall- Renishaw Park, Chesterfield
- Royal standard pub beaconsfield
- Ruthin Gaol
- Salmesbury Hall - Lancashire
- Saltmarshe hall hotel - Howden
- Screaming woods,Pluckley kent uk
- Speke Hall - Merseyside
- St.Ediths church Shockach
- Stanhope St - Long Eaton
- Stocksbridge bypass "the most haunted road" in Britain.
- The bate hall hotel macclesfield
- The Crown Inn- Penn- Buckinghamshire
- The hellfire caves, Church Ln, West Wycombe, High Wycombe
- The mill of the black monks
- The new inn, 16 Northgate Street, Gloucester, England
- The village - Mansfield, Nottinghamshire
- Theatre Royal Drury Lane
- Tower of London - London
- Undercleve house
- Village of Pluckley - Kent
- Weir mill stockport
- Whitby Abbey,Abbey Ln, Whitby
- Woodchester Mansion - Nympsfield, Stonehouse, Gloucestershire

Sample below: *Name and Google earth X and Y co-ordinance with line of sight distance in meters, Line of sight meaning "the direct path between A and B".*

Name	X start	y start	GID st	Name	X end	y end	Line of Sight distance
30 east drive	-1.29406	53.68725	1	Borley Rectory	0.694054963	52.0544961	225706.6537
39 de grey street hull	-0.35338	53.76276	1	Borley Rectory	0.694054963	52.0544961	202798.0716
50 berkley square london	-0.14325	51.50781	1	Borley Rectory	0.694054963	52.0544961	83897.19443
Athelhampton House- Dorset	-2.32584	50.7489	1	Borley Rectory	0.694054963	52.0544961	255564.9691
Barcaldine Castle	-5.40156	56.51054	1	Borley Rectory	0.694054963	52.0544961	634821.7713
Beeston: (Nottinghamshire) - Crown Inn	-1.21572	52.93482	1	Borley Rectory	0.694054963	52.0544961	161877.9835
Belgrave Hall	-1.1251	52.65947	1	Borley Rectory	0.694054963	52.0544961	141035.4807
Berry Pomeroy Castle- Devon	-3.69609	50.449	1	Borley Rectory	0.694054963	52.0544961	351085.5621
black boy inn cvernafon	-4.27535	53.14119	1	Borley Rectory	0.694054963	52.0544961	357712.6184
Bolling Hall- bradford	-1.79893	53.77887	1	Borley Rectory	0.694054963	52.0544961	252176.9619
bradgate park- leicestershire	-1.20376	52.68828	1	Borley Rectory	0.694054963	52.0544961	147237.6089
Brislington	-2.54466	51.43963	1	Borley Rectory	0.694054963	52.0544961	234016.1801
buckfastleigh church devon	-3.77596	50.49273	1	Borley Rectory	0.694054963	52.0544961	356956.1748
Buckland Abbey- Yelverton	-4.1323	50.48137	1	Borley Rectory	0.694054963	52.0544961	379492.8392
cannock chase	-1.98589	52.7183	1	Borley Rectory	0.694054963	52.0544961	196832.8549
Cark (Cumbria)	-2.97792	54.18122	1	Borley Rectory	0.694054966	52.0544961	341151.5068
Chenies Manor House	-0.53928	51.67447	1	Borley Rectory	0.694054963	52.0544961	94527.34553
Chenies Manor House	-0.58327	51.67447	1	Borley Rectory	0.694054963	52.0544961	94527.04126
Chequers Inn. 51 London Road West- Amersham	-0.60701	51.66436	1	Borley Rectory	0.694054963	52.0544961	99581.27629
Chillingham Castle- Northumberland	-1.90384	55.52586	1	Borley Rectory	0.694054963	52.0544961	422528.7156
chingle hall	-2.67434	53.81621	1	Borley Rectory	0.694054963	52.0544961	299482.8694
Cock Lane	-0.70808	51.62768	1	Borley Rectory	0.694054963	52.0544961	107670.5225
Crown Inn - Church St- Beeston	-1.21572	52.92482	1	Borley Rectory	0.694054963	52.0544961	161877.9335

Then, I ran the following Query within the application, this will find the line of sight distance between each point and

DECLARE @source geography = 'POINT(0 51.5)'

DECLARE @target geography = 'POINT(-3 56)'

SELECT @source.STDistance(@target)

SELECT

> *Locations2.[GID start]*
> *,UK1.[Name]*
> *,Locations2.[X start]*
> *,Locations2.[y start]*
> *,Locations2.[GID end]*
> *,UK2.[Name]*
> *,Locations2.[X end]*
> *,Locations2.[y end]*
> *,Locations2.[Start].STDistance(Locations2.[End])*

FROM

> *SELECT Locations.*

,CAST('POINT(' + Locations.[X start] + ' ' + Locations.[y start] + ')' AS geography) [Start]

CAST('POINT(' + Locations.[X end] + ' ' + Locations.[y end] + ')' AS geography) [End]

FROM

    SELECT MP1.GID [GID start]

    ,MP1.X [X start]

    ,MP1.Y [y start]

    ,MP2.GID [GID end]

    ,MP2.X [X end]

    ,MP2.Y [y end]

    FROM [dbo].[uk] MP1

    CROSS JOIN

    [dbo].[uk] MP2

    WHERE MP1.GID <> MP2.GID

) Locations

) Locations2

INNER JOIN

    [dbo].[UK] AS [uk1]

        on Locations2.[GID start] = UK1.[GID]

INNER JOIN

    [dbo].[UK] AS [uk2]

        on Locations2.[GID end] = UK2.[GID]

ORDER BY Locations2.[GID start], Locations2.[GID end]

The result set was interesting, as it found that out of 69 of 79 locations (92%) were within 25 miles of each other.

Below, **on the far right, shows line of sight converted to miles.**

28	landbeach farm - sighting	0.162220858	52.26862612	23	Minster Tavern	0.262515714	52.89958546	16591.20869	10
28	landbeach farm - sighting	0.162220858	52.26862612	24	golden lion hotel-st ives	-0.066658637	52.34252567	17911.72938	11
28	landbeach farm - sighting	0.162220858	52.26862612	25	madingley hall- cambridge	0.054772222	52.24689114	7567.155057	5
28	landbeach farm - sighting	0.162220858	52.26862612	27	the new inn-st neots	-0.258310744	52.2422422	28857.38301	18
29	screaming woods	0.717887805	51.1651899	6	Village of Pluckley- Kent	0.756056888	51.17715486	2982.928591	2
30	Cark (Cumbria)	-2.977315998	54.181215	62	morecambe winter garden	-2.870981711	54.07126969	13977.72275	3
31	Beeston (Nottinghamshire) - Crown Inn	-1.2157166	52.924818	32	the village	-1.1943241	53.1428177	24382.92033	15
31	Beeston (Nottinghamshire) - Crown Inn	-1.2157166	52.924818	33	Stanhope St - Long Eaton- Nottingham NG10 4QN	-1.276731114	52.89962068	4971.01299	3
31	Beeston (Nottinghamshire) - Crown Inn	-1.2157166	52.924818	48	Belgrave Hall	-1.1250978	52.6594667	30155.03531	19
31	Beeston (Nottinghamshire) - Crown Inn	-1.2157166	52.924818	49	Nottingham galleries of justice	-1.1442029	52.95079	5608.982722	3
31	Beeston (Nottinghamshire) - Crown Inn	-1.2157166	52.924818	66	Old Victorian School Stanhope Street-Nottingham	-1.2763813	52.89957625	4954.402446	2
31	Beeston (Nottinghamshire) - Crown Inn	-1.2157166	52.924818	73	bradgate park- leicestershire	-1.203758473	52.68827894	26335.03682	16
32	the village	-1.1943243	53.1428177	31	Beeston (Nottinghamshire) - Crown Inn	-1.2157166	52.924818	24382.92033	15
32	the village	-1.1943243	53.1428177	33	Stanhope St - Long Eaton- Nottingham NG10 4QN	-1.276731114	52.89962068	27623.73814	17
32	the village	-1.1943243	53.1428177	39	Renishaw Hall	-1.344654894	53.30310088	20469.71556	13
32	the village	-1.1943243	53.1428177	49	Nottingham galleries of justice	-1.1442029	52.95079	21632.95785	19
32	the village	-1.1943243	53.1428177	66	Old Victorian School Stanhope Street-Nottingham	-1.2763813	52.89957625	27621.8923	17
33	Stanhope St - Long Eaton- Nottingham NG10 4QN	-1.276731114	52.89962068	31	Beeston (Nottinghamshire) - Crown Inn	-1.2157166	52.924818	4971.01299	3
33	Stanhope St - Long Eaton- Nottingham NG10 4QN	-1.276731114	52.89962068	32	the village	-1.1943243	53.1428177	27623.73814	17
33	Stanhope St - Long Eaton- Nottingham NG10 4QN	-1.276731114	52.89962068	48	Belgrave Hall	-1.1250978	52.6594667	28616.61084	18
33	Stanhope St - Long Eaton- Nottingham NG10 4QN	-1.276731114	52.89962068	49	Nottingham galleries of justice	-1.1442029	52.95079	10576.69103	7
33	Stanhope St - Long Eaton- Nottingham NG10 4QN	-1.276731114	52.89962068	66	Old Victorian School Stanhope Street-Nottingham	-1.2763813	52.89957625	30.05364214	0
33	Stanhope St - Long Eaton- Nottingham NG10 4QN	-1.276731114	52.89962068	73	bradgate park- leicestershire	-1.203758473	52.68827894	24026.2784	15
34	saltmarshe hall hotel	-0.8168447	53.7063428	19	30 east drive	-1.294080051	53.60724060	31651.46191	20
34	saltmarshe hall hotel	-0.8168447	53.7063428	20	35 degray street hull	-0.353870680	53.76275356	31228.80385	19
35	Kingsley House	-0.4082807	52.6815575	24	golden lion hotel-st ives	-0.066658637	52.34252567	39658.52704	25
35	Kingsley House	-0.4082807	52.6815575	26	peterborough museum	-0.243573374	52.57857396	12617.508	8
37	Brislington	-2.5466573	51.4398281	2	Ram Inn	-2.348083486	51.6379782	26035.60174	16
37	Brislington	-2.5466573	51.4398281	5	Woodchester Mansion- Gloucestershire	-2.277727112	51.7107569	35465.78882	22
38	Minsden Chapel-	-0.259566876	51.90691488	27	the new inn-st neots	-0.258310744	52.2422422	37311.48526	23
38	Minsden Chapel-	-0.259566876	51.90691488	40	The Chequers Inn-Amersham	-0.6070454	51.6645751	36082.71849	22
38	Minsden Chapel-	-0.259566876	51.90691488	68	Chenies Manor House	-0.5332744	51.6744742	32023.40808	30
39	Renishaw Hall	-1.344654894	53.30310088	32	the village	-1.1943243	53.1428177	20483.71556	13
39	Renishaw Hall	-1.344654894	53.30310088	59	stockbridge bypass	-1.5014337	53.4862078	28168.51694	16
39	Renishaw Hall	-1.344654894	53.30310088	60	the mill of the black monks	-1.4399627	53.551040	28388.33346	18
40	The Chequers Inn-Amersham	-0.6070454	51.6645751	21	Hampton Court Palace	-0.337763066	51.40361398	34526.97656	21
40	The Chequers Inn-Amersham	-0.6070454	51.6645751	38	Minsden Chapel-	-0.259566876	51.90691488	36082.71840	22
40	The Chequers Inn-Amersham	-0.6070454	51.6645751	41	Cock Lane	-0.7080504	51.6276772	8107.577974	5
40	The Chequers Inn-Amersham	-0.6070454	51.6645751	56	the hellfire caves	-0.8026169	51.6459504	13692.10064	9
40	The Chequers Inn-Amersham	-0.6070454	51.6645751	63	THEATRE ROYAL DRURY LANE- London	-0.12037151	51.51285361	37717.4111	23
40	The Chequers Inn-Amersham	-0.6070454	51.6645751	64	royal standard pub beaconsfield	-0.668092602	51.6186185	6660.045859	4
40	The Chequers Inn-Amersham	-0.6070454	51.6645751	65	The Crown Inn- Penn- Buckinghamshire	-0.695956363	51.63533776	6866.62518	4

40	The Chequers Inn-Amersham	-0.6070454	51.6645751	68	Chenies Manor House	-0.5332744	51.6744742	5221.15789	3
40	The Chequers Inn-Amersham	-0.6070454	51.6645751	78	50 berkley square london	-0.1432546	51.5078071	35572.12365	23
41	Cock Lane	-0.7080504	51.6276772	21	Hampton Court Palace	-0.337763066	51.40361398	35807.04204	22
41	Cock Lane	-0.7080504	51.6276772	40	The Chequers Inn Amersham	-0.6070454	51.6645751	8107.577974	5
41	Cock Lane	-0.7080504	51.6276772	56	the hellfire caves	-0.8026169	51.6459504	6855.47214	4
41	Cock Lane	-0.7080504	51.6276772	64	royalstandard pub beaconsfield	-0.668092602	51.6186185	2985.02751	2
41	Cock Lane	-0.7080504	51.6276772	65	The Crown Inn- Penn- Buckinghamshire	-0.695956363	51.63533776	1194.854434	1
41	Cock Lane	-0.7080504	51.6276772	68	Chenies Manor House	-0.5332744	51.6744742	13186.33421	8
43	RAF Bircham Newton	0.6622704	52.87432955	44	Raynham Hall-	0.7902453	52.7963646	12233.50477	6
44	Raynham Hall-	0.7902453	52.7963646	43	RAF Bircham Newton	0.6622704	52.87432955	12233.50477	8
45	Edge Hill-- southern Warwickshire	-1.4556267	52.1238445	46	Ettington Park	-1.640099445	52.1237384	12634.24821	8
46	Ettington Park	-1.640099445	52.1237384	45	Edge Hill-- southern Warwickshire	-1.4556267	52.1238445	12634.24821	8
48	Belgrave Hall	-1.1250978	52.6594667	31	Beeston (Nottinghamshire) - Crown Inn	-1.2157166	52.924818	30155.03531	19
48	Belgrave Hall	-1.1250978	52.6594667	33	Stanhope St - Long Eaton- Nottingham NG10 4QN	-1.276731114	52.89962068	28616.61084	18
48	Belgrave Hall	-1.1250978	52.6594667	49	Nottingham galleries of justice	-1.1442029	52.95079	32444.80575	20
48	Belgrave Hall	-1.1250978	52.6594667	66	Old Victorian School Stanhope Street-Nottingham	-1.2763813	52.89957625	28603.56236	18
48	Belgrave Hall	-1.1250978	52.6594667	73	bradgate park- leicestershire	-1.203758473	52.68827894	6212.121617	4
49	Nottingham galleries of justice	-1.1442029	52.95079	31	Beeston (Nottinghamshire) - Crown Inn	-1.2157166	52.924818	5608.982722	3
49	Nottingham galleries of justice	-1.1442029	52.95079	32	the village	-1.1943243	53.1428177	21632.95785	13
49	Nottingham galleries of justice	-1.1442029	52.95079	33	Stanhope St - Long Eaton- Nottingham NG10 4QN	-1.276731114	52.89962068	10576.69103	7
49	Nottingham galleries of justice	-1.1442029	52.95079	48	Belgrave Hall	-1.1250978	52.6594667	32444.80575	20
49	Nottingham galleries of justice	-1.1442029	52.95079	66	Old Victorian School Stanhope Street-Nottingham	-1.2763813	52.89957625	10559.34491	7
49	Nottingham galleries of justice	-1.1442029	52.95079	73	bradgate park- leicestershire	-1.203758473	52.68827894	29442.60503	19
50	llangelynnin church	-3.8729855	53.2458307	61	black boy inn caernafon	-4.275748763	53.14118651	29333.40735	13
50	llangelynnin church	-3.8729855	53.2458307	74	Ruthin Gaol	-3.318827096	53.11388591	40161.88147	25
51	st.ediths church shockach	-2.848683401	53.0456579	15	Speke Hall- Liverpool- Merseyside	-2.87352903	53.33649732	32430.22513	20
51	st.ediths church shockach	-2.848683401	53.0456579	17	Plas Teg- Mold- Flintshire	-3.0670971	53.1296513	17867.87892	11
51	st.ediths church shockach	-2.848683401	53.0456579	53	Hack Green Secret Nuclear Bunker- French Lane- Nantwich	-2.5305021	53.0272832	21448.39719	13
51	st.ediths church shockach	-2.848683401	53.0456579	74	Ruthin Gaol	-3.313027006	53.11388591	32085.52030	20
52	weir mill stockport	-2.166580921	53.40888359	57	the bate hall hotel macclesfield	-2.127353677	53.26087827	16677.86742	10
52	weir mill stockport	-2.166580921	53.40888359	58	ordsall hall manchester	-2.277508968	53.46988385	9983.683827	6
52	weir mill stockport	-2.166580921	53.40888359	59	stockbridge bypass	-1.5914337	53.4862078	39170.25859	24
53	Hack Green Secret Nuclear Bunker- French Lane- Nantwich	-2.5305021	53.0272832	17	Plas Teg- Mold- Flintshire	-3.0670971	53.1296513	37722.14884	23
53	Hack Green Secret Nuclear Bunker- French Lane- Nantwich	-2.5305021	53.0272832	51	st.ediths church shockach	-2.848683401	53.0456579	21448.39719	13
53	Hack Green Secret Nuclear Bunker- French Lane- Nantwich	-2.5305021	53.0272832	57	the bate hall hotel macclesfield	-2.127353677	53.26087827	37465.15845	23
54	Edinburgh Vaults	-3.18738489	55.94912206	55	mary kings close	-3.1904556	55.9498297	207.3893158	0
55	mary kings close	-3.1904556	55.9498297	54	edinburgh Vaults	-3.18738489	55.94912206	207.3893158	0
56	the hellfire caves	-0.8026169	51.6459504	40	The Chequers Inn Amersham	-0.6070454	51.6645751	13692.10064	9
56	the hellfire caves	-0.8026169	51.6459504	41	Cock Lane	-0.7080504	51.6276772	6855.47214	4
56	the hellfire caves	-0.8026169	51.6459504	64	royal standard pub beaconsfield	-0.668092602	51.6186185	9758.722354	6
56	the hellfire caves	-0.8026169	51.6459504	65	The Crown Inn- Penn- Buckinghamshire	-0.695956363	51.63533726	7477.557557	5
56	the hellfire caves	-0.8026169	51.6459504	68	Chenies Manor House	-0.5332744	51.6744742	18005.88531	12

So what does this mean?

Above dataset mapped

And a pattern becomes clear

Mapped below are the buildings / houses that **so active** it is impossible to live in one full time,

Observe the locations within the highlighted area - with similar "point-to-point distances"

Or clusters

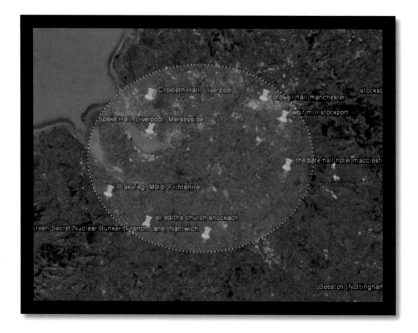

Conclusion

According to: *https://insidemystery.com/oddities/ley-lines-and-why-people-think-they-hold-supernatural-energy*

- *In 1921, the theory of ley lines was developed by Alfred Watkins, an amateur archaeologist.*
- *Watkins theorized that there are lines of low-frequency energy all over the world that crisscross each other. Along these lines are monuments and natural landforms.*
- *Watkins believed that these lines carried supernatural energy and low-frequency vibrations.*

Noun: ley line

- *A supposed straight line connecting three or more prehistoric or ancient sites, sometimes regarded as the line of a former track and associated by some with lines of energy and other paranormal phenomena.*

However that doesn't explain the 11 till 3 am time pattern or witching hours (known to be the most active period of the night) or the similar point to point distances between active locations. The reality is if these ley lines were responsible for paranormal activity, the public would observe activity **all the time** and not **only certain hours of the night.**

Technical observation: The patterns mapped could only be described as a **network** with **occasional minor variation.**

- These areas have been observed to become more active from around 11pm to 3am
- Each location is similar distance (approx 20 miles) to the next operating in lines or clusters as shown above

This logically indicates there is a **relationship** between these **extremely active** sites; meaning there is an overall **system** at work.

- Logically - to control or use this system two data communication processes would need to be in operation , firstly the primary data mechanism would be required to **emit** a downward looking **control / communication signal**
- **While** a secondary **local broadcast** communication system would be used to relay data short distances between each site.
- This would explain the similar distances between locations, as each sphere is working as a **node**—In theory this could be a **point to point communication** system in action,

The patterns indicate a **low to ground network** is in operation, and is technically similar to the network topology of a **microwave based point to point communication relay system** - microwaves because only microwaves can travel in straight lines, logically it could be the case that it uses microwaves for long distance transmission and digital UHF / Radio transmissions for short range (local) transmissions.

With each location operating at a similar distance to the next and each location could be what one could describe as a hard node. Meaning, in order for the rest of the network to operate, the sphere needs to be assigned to that location. The hard nodes are "active" meaning they don't only broadcast signals to each other in the chain, but also to and from to the surrounding spheres directly above them – **in other words this appears to be a stealthy ground based communication network** relaying signals from the sky above and pushing the signal / data across the country, **same process as our satellite communication network but operating in reverse.**

- **This is consistent with the analyses from** Dr. Carl Wilson of the Omega Minus One Institute mentioned earlier in the book stating *"this object (sphere) is emitting radio waves"*
- This could be why new homes or buildings with no history can become extremely active all of a sudden. It depends on if the network shifts, resulting in old active areas ceasing to be active and new selected areas becoming active. With this logic, it would conclude that paranormal activity *has nothing to do with human death rates or human history*. This perception is an understandable human error caused by misidentification of the phenomena.
- This would explain the non-human like behaviour pattern of paranormal activity, as these spheres could only be controlled and managed by one thing and that is - Artificial intelligence

- From my own tests and reading 3rd party accounts, it would appear this artificial intelligence is designed to observe and mimic basic human interaction, providing only very basic communication, relaying basic messages via directed radio broadcast creating EVPs – picked up as cross talk on circuits. Or by Audio via air by resonating its propulsion field creating force on air – creating sound waves

- This could be why during spirit box session's intelligent answers are received in a number of different voices. When people are asking questions, it queries a central database where a direct answer is relayed from a library of voice samples. But like all database technologies, one has to be very specific in the query (or question). Hence why one moment the investigator is getting answers and the next it stops— the question is not understood or it isn't referenced within the database.

Now, if these objects are broadcasting signals there is a good chance these transmissions/signal type or frequencies would have a negative effect on human health. Even our normal transmitter technology used in telecoms and microwave data links have health impacts in very close proximity; hence it is common that these powerful transmitters are mounted high off the ground to take full advantage of the Inverse-Square Law of Propagation.

This would certainly explain the common paranormal hangover I myself and many have suffered. Up close, this microwave based / electronic emissions could create a form of radiation poisoning that would have a negative electrical impact on our bio-chemical/electrical processes within our nervous system and brain. If this is correct, other paranormal behaviour traits start to become understandable. The same way we would throw stones at a bunch of stray animals that are lurking in dangerous areas

These spheres perform the same action to push us away from dangerous broadcast zones using either direct or indirect tactics.

During my research at 30 East Drive, I was in very close proximity to these spheres. When the objects would engage directly, the sphere would use its field-based propulsion system to create force on objects such as walls or doors. This would create a banging effect and/or or project small objects (such as marbles) at speed toward people or other objects.

Indirect actions are a more common sphere behaviour, and look and feel different than a direct action, meaning actions that are not directly forced on you, but forces you to refocus ones attention to a different part of the building or area, while a direct action would cause a physical impression – a push – scratch or impact For example, if the sphere needs to broadcast upstairs and someone is in that area, the object performs an indirect action downstairs. This will attract that person to take a look, and while the person is downstairs (and outside of the immediate broadcast zone), the sphere can uplink and broadcast safely. In other words, the spheres use indirect tactics to move people around - to create space

Now while that works in principle, the reality is 21st century paranormal investigators are stubborn; mainstream investigators will stick around high activity locations, and/or spread out throughout the location. This results in these spheres performing forced uplinks— meaning transmissions while people are in close proximity. Forced uplinks result in a possible exposure to a very high dose of electromagnetic radiation. Chronic exposure to electromagnetic radiation produces widespread neuropsychiatric effects including depression. This consistent, long-term exposure could also explain why those who are sadly stuck and forced to live in these active areas typically start to suffer from mental health issues.

Reference: Professor Emeritus of Biochemistry and Basic Medical Sciences, Washington State University)

Source:

https://www.sciencedirect.com/science/article/pii/S0891061815000 599

Reference: *Yan-Hui Hao, Biological effects of MW radiation, Beijing Institute of Radiation Medicine, Beijing, 100850 China*

Source: *https://www.ncbi.nlm.nih.gov/pmc/articles/PMC4440565/*

The biological effects of MW radiation fall into two types: thermal and non-thermal effect. Both are present, with thermal effects prominent in the case of high-power and high-frequency MW radiation and non-thermal effects predominant in the case of low-power MW radiation. MW radiation has multi-faceted effects on many systems within an organism, including the nervous, endocrine, cardiovascular, immune, reproductive and hematopoietic systems. The brain always requires a high rate of oxygen and energy consumption to maintain regular functions. Therefore, this organ is sensitive to non-infectious stimuli such as ionizing radiation and hypoxia. Research from our group and from others has demonstrated that microwave radiation damages hippocampal structures in rats, impairs long-term potentiation, decreases neurotransmitter concentrations, reduces synaptic vesicles in number and results in memory impairment. Thus, the brain is generally accepted as the most sensitive target organ for MW radiation.

The damaging effects of MW radiation on the brain include brain dysfunction and brain structural damage. An epidemiological survey found that MW radiation caused human fatigue, headache, excitement, dreams, memory loss and other symptoms of neurasthenia. In addition, there were impaired learning and memory abilities in rats after MW radiation, as determined by the Morris water maze. MW radiation may also lead to neuronal shrinkage, nuclear condensation, mitochondrial swelling, an expanded endoplasmic reticulum, alterations to the synaptic gaps and widened vascular endothelial connections, where mitochondrial injury occurred earlier and more severely.

During my research at 30 East Drive, we picked up high-frequency digital signals on a number of recorders. However, this signal wasn't constant but intermittent; a sporadic signal indicates this communication system is using a point-to-point burst transmission protocol. This means the sphere receives a signal, which it then rebroadcasted, and is subsequently relayed to the next sphere in the communication line.

Point-to-point burst transmission protocol would also explain why 30 East Drive is so active at its location. The home is located is the centre between two halves of the country, meaning it could be a very busy line. With Lots of up-linking equating to lots of broadcasting, which equates to lots of emissions, which ultimately results in lots of actions to keep people out of harm's way.

Reference: *Inventor: Maiyuran Wijayanathan, Noushad Naqvi,Hugh Hind*

Data Burst Communication Techniques For Use In Increasing Data Throughput To Mobile Communication Devices

Source: https://patents.google.com/patent/US20090034506

- *In telecommunication, a burst transmission or data burst is the broadcast of a relatively high-bandwidth transmission over a short period.*

- *Burst transmission can be intentional, broadcasting a compressed message at a very high data signalling rate within a very short transmission time. This technique is popular with the military and spies, who both wish to minimize the chance of their radio transmissions being detected, a low probability of intercept (LPI) and low probability of recognition (LPR).*

- *In the 1980s, the term "data burst" (and "info burst") was used for a technique used by some United Kingdom and South African TV programmes to transmit large amounts of primarily textual information. They would display multiple pages of text in rapid succession, usually at the end of the programme; viewers would videotape it and then read it later by playing it back using the pause button after each page.*

Why would these spheres broadcast from inside buildings?

This could be due to the "Inverse-Square Law of Propagation"

Reference: https://www.gb.nrao.edu/GBTopsdocs/primer/inverse-square_law_of_propa.htm

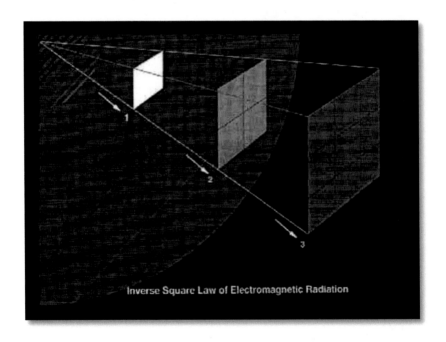

Inverse Square Law of Electromagnetic Radiation

Reference: *http://hyperphysics.phy-astr.gsu.edu/hbase/Forces/isq.html*

- *Inverse-Square Law of Propagation. As electromagnetic radiation leaves its source, it spreads out, travelling in straight lines, as if it were covering the surface of an ever-expanding sphere. This area increases proportionally to the square of the distance the radiation has travelled*

With the Inverse-Square Law of Propagation in mind, we can explain why these spheres choose to broadcast from inside buildings. The first reason been the building materials themselves would help shield the surrounding population from possible mutagenesis effects. Absorbing the stray electronic signatures and resulting by-product physical effects on the human body. The second reason could be directly related, by masking the electronic signatures and blending in with background electromagnetic radiation / noise this reduced vertical detection from above by a 3rd party – what is presented - is a stealthy low-to-ground communication network using burst transmissions

The diagram below shows how these hard nodes connect between locations. When messages or commands are sent, it runs though the chain—one performs a burst transmission—then the next sphere in line receives that data and relays it. Could this be the alien internet that was described in the 2017 documentary *Patient Seventeen*? In the film, a surgeon Dr. Roger Leir was removing alleged alien implants from human subjects for analysis. The implants were described as "emitting a signal and fused with human nerves", if this is the case; it means those implanted, would be subject to neural data mining / monitoring and real time tracking, it also means these implants must be linking to a local network.

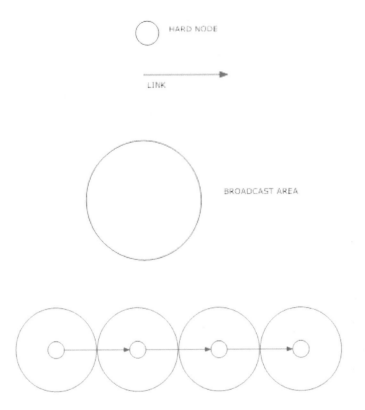

HARD NODE

LINK

BROADCAST AREA

Mapped below are reported to be buildings / homes that are so active, people can't live in them, five of these sites are approx 20 miles apart in lines or clusters.

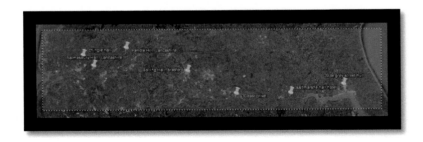

To compare our own computer networking we use something called *Point-to-Point Protocol or (PPP)*

This is what's known as a data link layer (layer 2) communications protocol, used to establish a direct connection between two nodes.

Reference:

https://www.juniper.net/documentation/en_US/junos/topics/topic-map/layer-2-understanding.html#id-ethernet-switching-and-layer-2-transparent-mode-overview

- *Layer 2, also known as the Data Link Layer, is the second level in the seven-layer OSI reference model for network protocol design. ... Layer2 is the network layer used to transfer data between adjacent network nodes in a wide area network or between nodes on the same local area network*

POINT TO POINT telecommunications, explained

> *Reference: https://en.wikipedia.org/wiki/Point-to-point_(telecommunications)*

- *"In telecommunications, a point-to-point connection refers to a communications connection between two Communication endpoints or nodes. An example is a telephone call, in which one telephone is connected with one other, and what is said by one caller can only be heard by the other. This is contrasted with a point-to-multipoint or broadcast connection, in which many nodes can receive information transmitted by one node. Other examples of point-to-point communications links are leased lines, microwave radio relay and two-way radio."*
- *"The term is also used in computer networking and computer architecture to refer to a wire or other connection that links only two computers or circuits, as opposed to other network topologies such as buses or crossbar switches which can*

connect many communications devices."

The only way a system like this would operate would be via directed microwaves, in many respects like our cellular network with a number of base stations waiting for someone's cellular phone to come in range and connect.

This would mean whatever is linking with this communication system **must be operating in the sky above**, transmitting downwards – in effect a **Line of sight** communication platform allowing long distance data relaying with very low probability of detection. This airborne system appears to be operating in a **geosynchronous orbit** which follows the 11pm to 3am time slot around the earth otherwise known as the **witching hours**. The spheres operating in the buildings would need to be autonomous using the same AI programming - with each containing the same behaviours and triggers, hence explaining why paranormal behaviour and effects are generally the same worldwide, this means the same mechanisms are in use and were all created by the same source. The Spheres would be required to self organise - by what we call "AI Swarm intelligence"

Reference: https://en.wikipedia.org/wiki/Swarm_intelligence

- *Swarm intelligence (SI) is the collective behaviour of decentralized, self-organized systems, natural or artificial. The concept is employed in work on **artificial intelligence.***

Swarm intelligence allows an **adaptive network that can change and reconfigure to its needs**. In this case the network shifts, new areas are selected and become active. While the previous areas stop, explaining the fact that 'mathematically' paranormal activity generally remains at the same low level, but it's observed to move around.

PART TWELVE

QUICK OVERVIEW OF CURRENT ANALYSIS

Let's back up—so far we have identified an artificial object operating in 30 East Drive, whereas the object size/flight characteristics general appearance and physical abilities match the Foo-Fighter object observed during World War II.

As mentioned earlier in the book these Spheres have been found and analysed by US Navy scientists and said to have an atomic number of approximately 150 plus, meaning that these objects can't be physically replicated. This book has mathematically demonstrated that constant paranormal activity isn't in any way related to human death rates. I have also made scientific arguments that debunk stone tape and current EVP theory. Also a pattern has been found between active locations, which are presenting a network topology of a high frequency dynamic network using a burst transmission protocols. I then explained the possible side effects of being in close proximity, hence presenting a solid reason paranormal-like action are used to force people away from such areas. This also covers why new buildings with no history become active as the dynamic network can shift from one location to another.

- **These active homes/areas are hard nodes, in effect; relay stations creating the underlining infrastructure of this system which uplinks when required.**
- **This emission issue explains why they use the inside of**

buildings to broadcast from—as the building materials would help shield the outside world/people from harmful effects and even detection.

These spheres would all be coded with the same programming, based on the observation they share the same behaviour traits (the most common being the cat-and-mouse pattern).

- Intense activity is generally located in two areas —the top floor / attic of a building or the basement of the same building. In other words, they broadcast from areas that are within the confines of the structure but as far away from human contact as possible.

- Generally if the person is on the ground floor activity will occur upstairs and if a person went upstairs, then activity would subsequently start occurring downstairs (and vice versa) this behaviour implies these objects are moving people around creating space between them and the transmissions

As mentioned, this behaviour doesn't replicate human behaviour logic. As humans we generally desire to be connected to groups, are social and status-seeking animals. While this Sphere's exhibit behaviour of avoidance with limited interaction and intermittent physical actions.

- The social isolation of these spheres from humans and/or other spheres would allow continuous broadcast. The desire to broadcast in seclusion has the side effect of creating a cat-and-mouse game; individuals are motivated by indirect actions to form groups, and in effect, under control and at a safe distance.

Below the "Hardnode" Sphere operating at 30 East Drive

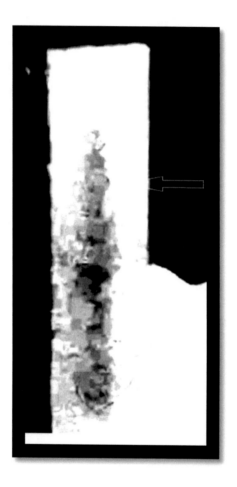

What are Environmental Spheres?

While these Type 3 (hard node) spheres are operating as a relay, they are broadcasting and remaining in the same general area—the surrounding Type 2 environmental spheres are exactly the same object but operating in a quantum state outside of our visual capability's. Environmental spheres appear to receive commands while moving freely from area to area. From what I can tell, they are mostly monitoring areas of genetic interest, meaning areas with high concentration of human DNA and other areas of naturally evolving genetic resource. They appear to operate in a passive state creating very little paranormal like activity, however. These environmental spheres appear be detectable and track able by the vertical high voltage static fields they emit, also they appear to be **visible under strong directed IR light**, and these will appear via Gen 2 / 3 night vision cameras **as transparent /or small solid sphere objects.**

Reference:

https://www.youtube.com/watch?v=qnJp_ttzOfc&feature=youtu.be &fbclid=IwAR1_U3pT9-oUjqvqKA4OStH8IRN4GV34AYYKwhhkxjzjMNItfL7h5xr49BI

Below, *these spheres can be seen close up with Gen 2 / 3 night vision cameras, but invisible to the naked eye*

In order to test this hypothesis I needed to find an area that showed no activity during the day but appeared to come active at night

- My hypothesis would need to be tested in a public area—where the passive spheres are free to roam and observe.

To test out my idea, I went to meet Mike in Manchester to film an episode of UHUK.

Aug Sat 11th 2018

Ultimate Haunted UK Episode Apethorn Lane Crazy Activity

In this demonstration, we have a number of vertical static detectors and other devices placed on a table within a known active tunnel in Apethorn Lane, Manchester. We tested the location during the day at approximately 2pm and no detections were identified.

We headed down again around 11pm and setup by 11:30PM. Set-up including static detectors running down the centre line of the table and also placed on the table perimeter spaced equally apart. As expected multiple vertical static fields were detected within minutes. That same small area that **during the day** was **not-active became active during the night. During these detections, EVPs were heard and recorded on the camera. What were noticeable** were the sensors, tracking different directions at once. This could indicate that there was not one **source,** but multiple **separate vertical static sources** interacting with each detector. **Instant acceleration** was also observable from these sources, from left to right within half a second; this is a known trait of a field-based propulsion system and commonly observed in UFO reports and videos.

Notice the detectors below: One in the centre is tracking a source directly above it, while the two on the right are tracking a source to its far right.

What was observable was the detectors were tracking multiple sources that appeared to be slowly circling us.

As mentioned above, if these are networked drone-type objects, they will work within a swarm. Thus, a number of spheres will turn up at once with each emitting their own separate vertical static fields. The video stills demonstrate separate detectors lighting up and then turning off independently, only then to leave all at once

A number of EVPs were recorded on camera simultaneous to the detection of these multiple static fields. It would appear that these spheres when in close proximity to people trigger, and start communicating / creating a basic human interaction via broadcasting directed radio transmissions at the cameras and other recording devices, these transmissions are picked up as electronic crosstalk and recorded on the device, this is a mechanism is explained later in the book.

The behaviour observed in the tunnel demonstrates a dynamic network in action; a hard node underlining network which controls a passive swarm of silver sphere drones that are operating in a quantum / stealth state. Although near invisible to the human eye, the spheres can be tracked by the high voltage vertical static emissions. As mentioned these objects seem to be monitoring certain areas of genetic resources.

Reference: *https://www.wipo.int/tk/en/genetic/*

- *Genetic resources (GRs) refer to genetic material of actual or potential value. Genetic material is any material of plant, animal, microbial or other origin containing functional units of heredity.*

- *Examples include material of plant, animal, or microbial origin, such as medicinal plants, agricultural crops and animal breeds*

The question that comes to mind is why? What's so special about woodlands or grave yards and other areas of genetic materials?

PART THIRTEEN

A POSSIBLE DEFENSIVE MEASURE?

During my research period I wondered if it was possible to counter these objects, as in push them away or force them to react in a way that could be detected. After thinking for a while, I figured that if these objects are designed to work at night, they could be using a passive infrared vision system. Such a system would capacitate spheres to see in darkness without emitting any infrared light. Passive IR vision is the primary visualization system of the stealth F-117 aircraft; to achieve stealth (to minimize detection by radar / IR technologies) no thermal evidence or infrared emission can be allowed to leave the craft. However, in the case of spheres, photons hit the surface to amplify visual data, subsequently allowing it to operate in low light/darkness.

If this was the case, then it may be possible to "blind" a sphere. I figured—if this is a machine—the inherent Artificial intelligence system would react in an unpredictable way if the sensor data becomes corrupted, thus "blind." Just like our modern computer-controlled-fly-by-wire aircrafts, when the external sensors fail they provide erroneous data. For a passenger aircraft, the flight computer **is defaulted to** make the craft act erratic when fed incorrect data. Failed or corrupted sensors are the cause of a number of fatal passenger aircraft crashes, resulting in a tragic loss of the many lives. A recent example of occurring is the two Boeing 737 MAX crashes in 2018 and 2019.

Reference:

https://en.wikipedia.org/wiki/Boeing_737_MAX_groundings

- *In March 2019, aviation authorities around the world grounded the Boeing 737 MAX passenger airliner after two new airplanes crashed within five months, killing all 346 people aboard. After the first accident, Lion Air Flight 610 on October 29, 2018, investigators suspected that the MAX's new Manoeuvring Characteristics Augmentation System (MCAS), which was omitted from flight manuals and crew training, automatically and repeatedly forced the aircraft to nosedive. In November 2018, Boeing and the U.S. Federal Aviation Administration (FAA) sent airlines urgent messages to emphasize a flight recovery procedure, and Boeing started to redesign MCAS. In December 2018, studies by the FAA and Boeing, publicized a year later, concluded that MCAS posed an unacceptable safety risk. On March 10, 2019, Ethiopian Airlines Flight 302 crashed, despite the crew's attempt to use the recovery procedure. The airline grounded its MAX fleet that day.*

Like all passive infrared vision systems, **intense bright light** can overwhelm the sensor and if that sensor is feeding a flight computer of some type (as described above) there is a good chance the software will go into a state of confusion and do something unexpected. I performed a test at 30 East Drive to try out this idea. The cameramen and I blacked out the rooms and deployed a filament based 240v strobe light. As the light turned on we monitored the electronic signals and sounds picked up by an array of microphones around the house;

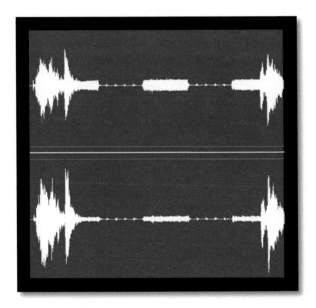

***The above was picked up by an array of microphones
placed around 30 East Drive:***

- The small ticks represent the strobe tick and the three larger

beeps (left – centre and last) are from the K2 meter
- Observe the pattern of three long detections
- Observe four pulses - and signal on for four—off for four on for four.

The moment this test started, every microphone in every room of 30 East Drive started receiving extreme signals at exactly the same time. Logically, we can argue this would have been a mix of electronic crosstalk and ultra high freq UHF sound waves emitted from the sphere as the AI drops into a state of error. The observed behaviour may demonstrate that once these objects are blinded - they drop into a state of error then perform a software / hardware reset.

What I believe we observed was a re-initialization process with digital signals emitted in a systematic way, **with the same time period** between each electronic transmission.

- "Systematic" - meaning - 'done or acting according to a fixed plan or system; methodical'. In the same way a mobile phone will reconnect to the carrier network.

Logically, this benchmark could be the uplink signal as it resets and reconnects to the network. By all accounts this is the behaviour of a machine and not a human spirit, suggesting the analyses could be correct. We can argue spheres **do operate** using a passive IR vision system, and when sensors are blinded the AI goes into a state of error. The behaviour of the ill-fated Boeing 737 MAX aircrafts with corrupted sensor data produced comparable results. This pattern supports the theory that **basic technical behaviour traits** remain the same, no matter how advanced the technology or the earthly or extra-terrestrial origin of the machine.

This **system reset** effect is interesting, as people who are unable to move out from an active location and could use this blinding method as a defence measure, thus pushing aggressive paranormal activity away when or if required

Logically if the sphere has problems operating in that area, it will put pressure on the network. Meaning—delayed or corrupted transmissions will occur, causing errors - all systems have an error threshold that once met the network will be forced to move, once the sphere moves that location will no longer be active. The other possible defensive measures could be with signal blockers—as long as you know the frequency the spheres are broadcasting on, the signal could be jammed. Again, this would put stress on the network, which will then hit an error threshold, and the sphere will be forced to move away.

PART FOURTEEN

HOW COULD THESE SPHERES CREATE POLTERGEIST ACTIVITY?

We know that poltergeist activity is defined as:

Objects moved/thrown/doors getting banged (see page #).

As these spheres are demonstrating a level of technology that we can't replicate, it is very possible that they are directed connected to the UFO phenomenon. Earlier in the book (pages # -#) there are images of hundreds of these sphere objects getting deployed from a larger object. If this is the case, then there is a good chance these spheres are using the same or very similar propulsion process / system & principles of the larger UFO "people" carrying type crafts. The now world famous nuclear physicist, Bob Lazar, went public during the late 1980s in regard to his reverse engineering work on the type of craft show below - a flying disk known as the sports model. This work was said to be carried out at a top secret base in Area 51, Nevada. Lazar described two main modes of flight: 1) Omicron Mode; and 2) Delta Mode. The question is—can these propulsion modes replicate observed paranormal actions such as banging and movement of objects?

Figure#8 Graphics from
http://www.gravitywarpdrive.com/Government_Scientist.htm

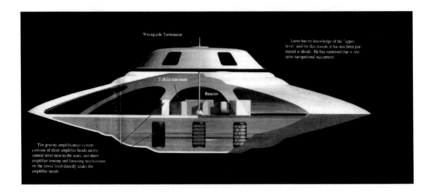

Figure#9

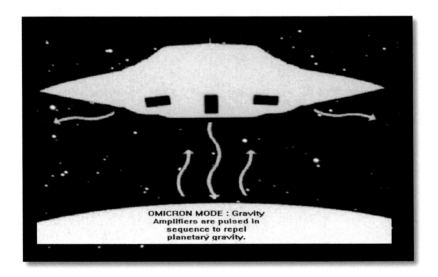

Figure #10

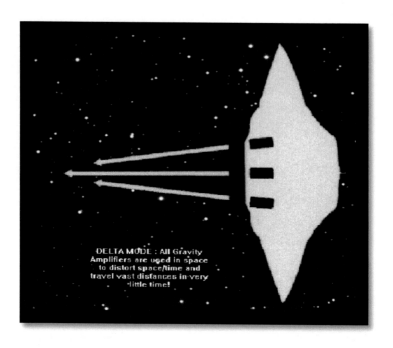

DELTA MODE : All Gravity
Amplifiers are used in space
to distort space/time and
travel vast distances in very
little time!

With these propulsion modes in mind it would appear that Omicron mode would be suitable to create such effects, to create force on a household object or surface such as a wall, it is a simple action. The sphere drop into Omicron Mode and focuses its two remaining amplifiers on to its target (such as a marble) creating force, hence making it move or fly at will. If this is indeed the case, it opens up some other possibilities as this projected force could be used to imitate a number of effects such as footsteps, banging on doors /walls, even creating scratching on walls.

The image below Number # is a video still taken at 30 East Drive at the very moment when a marble was fired towards the ground; notice the two lines / beams that is visible to the left of the ball. In order for a **glass marble** to be projected one needs to create force, the propulsion system from the craft above is said to be using directed gravitation waves which are vectored or guided by the three gravity amplifiers

Interestingly Bob Lazar performed a test on what he called the "gravity amplifiers."(As imaged above) Lazar performed a test by placing a burning candle underneath one of these amplifiers and as the amplifier was switched on—the candle *froze* in time - appearing like a photograph. This totally confused Lazar, as it flew in the face of known physics. But if this was the case, let's think about the behaviour:

1) The gravity amplifier is switched on;
2) Emits some kind of gravitational wave; and
3) The candle freezes in time.

This would indicate there is a mechanism where **gravity can slow time to the point of total stop.** Furthermore, altering the power of the wave could very well increase or decrease this effect on time. Thus, if the gravity amplifier was operating in a very low power state we would observe a slowing of light within the gravitational waves. In the experiment above it would appear the power level was sufficient to "lock time" in place.

Figure#11

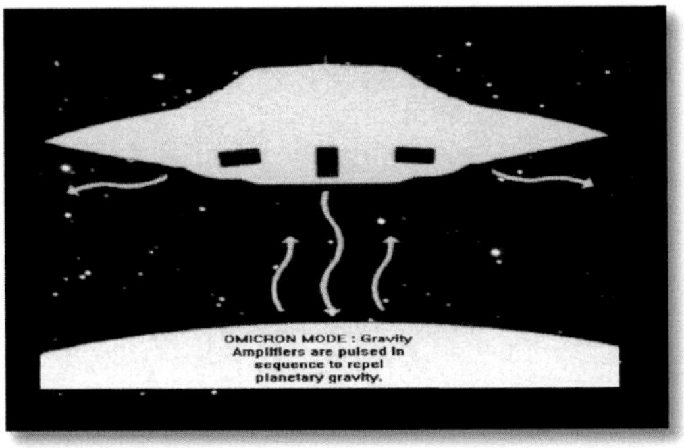

OMICRON MODE : Gravity Amplifiers are pulsed in sequence to repel planetary gravity.

Observe the two lines in the image below; this replicates Omicron mode, with one of the three gravity amplifier holding the sphere in place and the remaining two used for moving / projecting controlled force on objects. If this is the same process as the Lazar craft it would explain why we see two streaks of light. The same **mechanism produces the same behaviour and will ultimately slow down time within the beam.** Therefore the IR light emitting from the night vision camera is reflecting back from the beams - at a much slower speed; this slowed-down IR reflection is captured in the image as a pair of visibly elongated streaks of light.

Figure#12

Below: *Omicron Mode on the sphere platform - using one amplifier for propulsion, leaving two available for creating force on objects, resulting in two waves / beams observed during **poltergeist** activity*

Figure#13- Artists rendition

Observe the outline of the sphere with a single line of vertical force

Figure#14

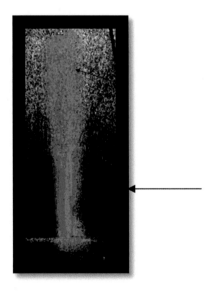

Figure#14b – Artists Rendition

PART FIFTEEN

WITH THIS ANALYSIS WHY CAN NORMAL HOUSEHOLD OBJECTS APPEAR TO TRIGGER PARANORMAL ACTIVITY?

Many people have visited areas of extreme activity and some have removed objects such as rocks / stones and other generic items from within them, while others have had these objects/ items brought into their home by accidental purchases, only to start experiencing strange paranormal events and effects

So what could be going on? Based on the behaviour traits of the observed spheres, spheres will avoid coming to into close contact with people (see page #) to create a buffer space between people and possibly mutagenic radiation/electronic burst UHF/microwave emissions.

Reference: https://en.wikipedia.org/wiki/Mutagen

- *In genetics, a mutagen is a physical or chemical agent that changes the genetic material, usually DNA, of an organism and thus increases the frequency of mutations above the natural background level. As many mutations can cause cancer, mutagens are therefore also likely to be carcinogens, although not always necessarily so. All mutagens have characteristic mutational signatures with some chemicals becoming mutagenic through cellular processes. Not all mutations are caused by mutagens: so-called "spontaneous mutations" occur due to spontaneous hydrolysis, errors in DNA replication, repair and recombination.*

What if there is a tertiary effect of radiation/emission exposure? And what if we can't yet detect these forces yet?

During an interview

Reference: *https://www.youtube.com/watch?v=XU7F1H6EzYs*

Boyd Bushman Lockheed Martin *Senior Scientist* mentioned

- *That by using Sir Isaac Newton created a form of mathematics called the binomial expansion where one can take any mathematics and put them into the expansion format, once added up you will get the correct definitions. Einstein's E = Mc is a binomial expression and if that is put into Newton's series expansion – and multiply it by m0c2 – mystically – the 1st term that is "1" **is a large force.** The 2nd is **Kinetic energy**; it goes on to show there **are eight significant forces.** The **first including the kinetic energy turns out to be the five we know.**

- *1: The Strong force (Atomic Binding – Gluons)*
- *2: Electromagnetism (Light – Photons)*
- *3: The Weak Force (W & Z Bosons)*
- *4: Gravity (Gravitons)*
- *5: Magnetism (Magnetic Force)*

- *The **sixth seventh and eighth** we don't know, but we believe Anti gravity is one of them*

If these spheres are using one of these "other" forces, then it's possible they emit a form of radiation that can't yet be detected.

Likewise, imagine if we gave a portable nuclear reactor to a group of 16th century scientists. The scientists investigate and start stripping the reactor down whiles its active; the absence of radioactive shielding does not cause them to feel any affects whatsoever of the exposure at the time. Fast forward and our irradiated folks begin to get sick and die. They have succumbed to a force that they can't detect, can't see, can't smell...

From my analysis it would suggest that advanced spheres are using an exotic field-based propulsion system, these spheres have been analysed and reported to have an atomic number of 140 to 150 operating well outside of our periodic table and material science;

It's very possible that our environment (stones and wood and other materials) can soak up and become contaminated by a type of radioactive by-product we simply can't detect, but nevertheless has negative long-term impacts on health and DNA.

When these contaminated objects are removed from active sites, it would be possible that the passive spheres could detect this type of radiation / emission from a far, on detection they head in and locate the source. This isn't a stretch as even our earthly Air force drones such as the Lockheed Martin RQ-170 Sentinel contains sensors that can monitor / analyse and identify airborne partials that contain chemical/ biological/ nuclear signatures at high altitude.

Figure#15 RQ-170 Sentinel

Those in possession of these contaminated objects / items would then experience paranormal activity around and local to the contaminated object / item itself - as the spheres engage, they will create scarecrow like effects within its proximity, thus explaining haunted dolls / ordainments and even furniture.

All these spheres are attempting to do is to keep people at a safe distance, from forces we yet fully understand, In many cases people have returned these unknowingly contaminated objects / items with letters of apology stating that whatever spirit was at the house followed them home and caused havoc.

Interestingly in some cases, it would appear that contaminated objects / items have been purposely buried or hidden within a location with malicious intent; so-called devil worship or pagan groups who have (and still operate) on the fringes of society are allegedly responsible. Although it's understandable that people over history have misinterpreted this paranormal phenomenon, it appears some fringe groups in Witchcraft / Black Magic or Voodoo have observed this contamination behaviour trait and used it for their own advantage.

Reference:

https://unsolvedmysteries.fandom.com/wiki/Tallman_House

Tallman House

Horicon, Wisconsin

Date: May 1987 to January 1988

In early February of 1987, Allen and Deborah "Debbie" Tallman brought home a bunk bed that they purchased at a second hand shop. They assembled the bed and stored it in their basement. When the Tallmans moved the bed upstairs in May of 1987, it marked the beginning of nine months of horror for the family. From the moment the bed was first slept in, the house appeared to be haunted by spirits that terrorized first the children and then the entire family. The children, who were rarely sick before, suddenly became ill for no apparent reason. The night that the family moved the beds upstairs, their son "Danny" was in the room next to it. After his parents said goodnight to him, his clock radio apparently took on a life of its own. It turned itself on and randomly switched the channels under its own power. He reported that he saw the radio's vindicator moving itself. However, his parents did not believe him.

A few weeks later, Allen was painting the walls in his basement when he went up for lunch. He placed the paint brush on the table. When he returned, the brush was in the bucket with the bristles sticking up. When the youngest daughter was sleeping in the bunk bed, she claimed that she had seen a red-eyed witch behind her door. She also claimed that she saw fire in her room. A month later, Danny saw the same thing.

The family pastor was brought in, and he felt the presence of evil inside the house. The Tallmans continued to be tormented by the entities; doors would bang open and shut, strange voices would call out of nowhere, and ghostly visions persisted. A week before Christmas, Danny again saw something horrifying and told his mother that he wanted to leave. Frustrated, Allen told the spirits to get out of his house. He then said that if they wanted to fight someone, they could fight him. Three weeks later, at around 2AM on January 7, 1988, Allen returned home from the late shift. Outside the garage, he heard an eerie, howling sound, and went to investigate. A voice came out of the howling and said "come here". He went around the back to see if anyone was there, but there was no one. He then went back to the garage and saw that it was on fire. He went inside to get a fire extinguisher, but when he came back out, the fire was gone. The garage door was undamaged with no visible signs of recent fire consummation. When Allen got back inside, he went to reach for his lunch pail that he had set down, but the entity then threw it across the room.

Allen started sleeping in his daughters' room to provide protection. One night, a fog appeared around him. A voice came out of the fog that said "You're dead". Debbie then called the pastor because of what had happened to Allen. A few days later, Allen was working late and asked a relative to watch the girls. His relative was a complete skeptic, until that night. The same horrible figure seen by the children appeared, and he let out a loud scream. Debbie then told the relative to get the kids together, and that they were leaving the house forever.

Two weeks later, the Tallmans had the bunk beds destroyed. Afterwards, the Tallmans had no further paranormal experiences.

Note: That **once the bunk beds were destroyed no further paranormal activity occurred**; this is in line with the analysis above. Once an irradiated item has been destroyed, and/or removed from the area / away from the family—the spheres will disengage. The radiation is no longer a present danger, therefore the spheres will evacuate the area, and all sphere-driven paranormal activity will subsequently come to a halt. **However** if that item is later collected by someone else and again comes in close contact with people, activity **will start occurring again**... This suggests the spheres are monitoring from above - observing electronic / radioactive emissions using pattern analysis and comparison algorithms.

PART SIXTEEN

EVERYTHING HAS A REASON

With recent discoveries of other planets containing water and many other exotic minerals, the only true *unique resource* planet Earth harbours is that of **genetics.** The genetic resource of planet Earth has not been replicated on any planet we have currently discovered or observed from afar. Therefore it's possible that advanced external groups and interests would be interested in monitoring / extraction and control of access of such a rare asset. This control of access would also include protection; in the same way we protect key oil resources against 3rd party attacks, these spheres intercept hostile or unauthorised crafts / 3rd party groups and interests. The inherent value of green space or forestry could explain why spheres are seen cruising though woodlands as seen on page #.

Outside of the underlining hard node network, these active locations are generally found in areas of **high-genetic** value, meaning an area that is secluded but contains an abundance of naturally evolving DNA, be that plant life, animal life. However I believe the main resource attraction is that of human remains, and when one really thinks about it - a grave yard is a snapshot of human genetic history. As it's possible for us to extract the DNA from ancient dinosaur fossils then it's certainly possible to extract usable human genetic material from human remains - regardless if that material is fresh or hundreds of years old.

When one thinks about this—it does make sense. If an external force wanted hydrocarbons, then they would mine other planets like Jupiter, and likewise if they wanted heat they would use the Sun. According to NASA there is a massive asteroid 200km in diameter called 16 Psyche, this huge rock alone has so many heavy metals that its valued at £8,000 quadrillion, so logically speaking - space based mineral resource is more than plentiful.

The uncomfortable logic states **"we are the primary resource"** that is been monitored, most likely - we are having genetic material extracted, and like all resources - we are most likely tracked and sampled when required.

This includes areas of **high human concentration** be that Prisons - old people homes - hospitals etc

During my research, I spoke to a few people who worked in one of these locations, she mentioned that fast moving black masses are commonly seen in certain areas of the block and generally - when they are seen - people "pass away" in sets of threes.

The way an extraction system would work suggests the following model,

First these spheres perform surveys over a set of areas in which a number are selected,

Then genetic information is extracted from the environment and/or the human subjects.

As long as the monitored/extracted genetic resource does not drop below a certain threshold or capacity - the same areas will be observed/sourced from regardless of if they are in use or not.

This explains haunting and sightings within old prisons and grave yards that haven't been in use for decades. Areas that was once a concentrated genetic resource/interest—now derelict—but never the less **still monitored**, hence still active...

• Once the monitored/incoming genetic material has dropped

below the minimum capacity the spheres would **re-set** - a new survey is taken which **selects** new areas

- Once the new areas are found via a systemic survey. The whole network would have to adjust slightly for the change. Tiny changes might occur day-by-day while large changes might occur every few decades—hence buildings with no history can suddenly become active as the hard node network has shifted. In essence a sphere has entered a building and starts relaying data; the occupants of that building will then be on the receiving end of poltergeist activity as it performs actions to keep people at bay from microwaves and other electrical / radioactive by-products.

- Within this network there are three separate parts that allows this system to operate. The first part are the active spheres - these are acting as central communication relays, these are located in buildings and are the root cause of constant paranormal activity. This active network would **not be placed** in areas of genetic interest - but in an area **it needs to be** for the whole network to function. The second part is the same sphere drone but operating in a passive mode, these drones are monitoring/possibly extracting genetic material from preselected areas. And the third part is a high altitude airborne system (described next)

- This active network is using a burst broadcast communication method. These high energy transmissions (and possibly a radioactive by-product from the field-based propulsion system) produce long-term health affects in nearby biological life. As mentioned the spheres create actions to push people away when humans are in very close proximity, or when the sphere is about to broadcast. These actions range from simple knocking on walls, to direct transmission of images and sounds into the human target's visual cortex causing hallucinations (even on a group level).

It is a common biological practice on earth to protect a valuable resource from outside influence. If we extrapolate this practice to AI, we can explain why spheres engaged/tracked aircrafts during WW2. This behaviour is also seen today as with many UFO encounters/reports it's claimed that smaller sphere-like objects happen to turn up during large UFO events. I have termed this protective behaviour as a *firewall*, a concept leveraged from my IT background.

Reference:

https://www.cisco.com/c/en_uk/products/security/firewalls/what-is-a-firewall.html

- *A firewall is a network security device that monitors incoming and outgoing network traffic and decides whether to allow or block specific traffic based on a defined set of security rules.*

Or in this case a system that monitors incoming and outgoing air traffic, intercepting / controlling access to space or to the Earth

These are observed as spheres objects operating high in the sky - in lines or clusters

Reference:

https://www.youtube.com/watch?v=y7SBbpH2rhY&feature=youtu. be&fbclid=IwAR2ddtY2e7P-tqf4WlyuZPvKbWDahQK98L3r9ODiMylO_SXzDyj1L8a06yY

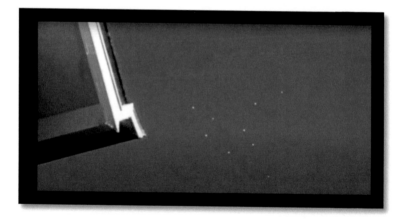

Below are three possible examples of this firewall type behaviour.

A great story that Quest TV and the BlackVault.com covered

Date of event 06/26/1959

Reference: *https://www.theblackvault.com/casefiles/father-gill-1959-papua-new-guinea-ufo-sighting/*

As indicated by his notes, Gill saw a bright white light in the north western sky. It appeared to be approaching the mission and hovering about 100 meters up. Eventually 38 people, including Gill, teachers Steven Gill Moi and Ananias Rarata, and Mrs Nessle Moi, gathered to watch the main UFO, which looked like a large, disc-shaped object. It was apparently solid and circular with a wide base and narrower upper deck. The object appeared to have four 'legs' underneath it. There also appeared to be about four 'panels' or 'portholes' on the side of the object, which seemed to glow a little brighter than the rest. At a number of intervals the object produced a shaft of blue light which shone upwards into the sky at an angle of about 45 degrees What looked like 'men' came out of the object, onto what seemed to be a deck on top of it. There were four men in all, occasionally two, then one, then three, then four. The shaft of blue light and the 'men' disappeared. The object then moved through some clouds. There were other UFO sightings during the night. Gill described the weather as variable sky scattered clouds to clear at first, becoming overcast after. He estimated the height of the clouds at about 600 meters. The first sighting over the sea, according to Rev. Gill, seemed to be about 150 metres above the water all times. The main UFO was clearly visible and seemed mostly stationary during the twenty-five minutes of observation. Astonishingly, the aerial visitor put in a repeat performance the following night, 27 June. Gill prepared another statement.

Large UFO first sighted by Annie Laurie at 6 p.m. in apparently same position as last night (26/6/59) only seemed a little smaller, when W.B.G. saw it at 6.02 p.m. I called Ananias and several others and we stood in the open to watch it. Although the sun had set it was still quite light for the following fifteen minutes. We watched figures appear on top four of them, no doubt that they are human. Possibly the same object that I took to be the "Mother" ship last night. Two smaller UFOs were seen at the same time, stationary.

One above the hills west, another over- head. On the large one two of the figures seemed to be doing something near the center of the deck, were occasionally bending over and raising their arms as though adjusting or "setting up" something (not visible). One figure seemed to be standing looking down at us (a group of about a dozen). I stretched my arm above my head and waved. To our surprise the figure did the same. Ananias waved both arms over his head then the two outside figures did the same. Ananias and self began waving our arms and all four now seemed to wave back. There seemed to be no doubt that our movements were answered. All mission boys made audible gasps (of either joy or surprise, perhaps both).

'As dark was beginning to close in, I sent Eric Kodawara for a torch and directed a series of long dashes towards the UFO. After a minute or two of this, the UFO apparently acknowledged by making several wavering motions back and forth. Waving by us was repeated and this followed by more flashes of torch, then the UFO began slowly to become bigger, apparently coming in our direction. It ceased after perhaps half a minute and came no further. After a further two or three minutes the figures apparently lost interest in us for they disappeared "below" deck. At 6.25 p.m. two figures re-appeared to carry on with whatever they were doing before the interruption. The blue spotlight came on for a few seconds twice in succession.'

Gill has described how he and the mission people called out to the men, even shouting at them, and beckoned them to descend, but there was no response beyond what has already been noted. Two smaller UFOs higher up remained stationary. By 6.30 p.m. the scene had remained largely unchanged, and Gill records that he went to dinner.

Figure#16 *[Images are CGI recreation from Quest TV]*

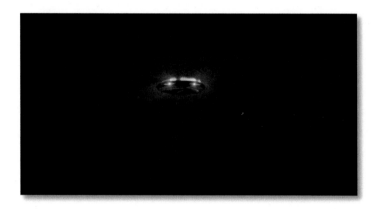

Father William Gill reported he witnessed two smaller sphere like UFOs come towards the craft and started circled the main craft.

__This is exactly the same behaviour traits as seen in WW2__, with the Airforce encountering the small silver spheres "foo-fighters". This engagement behaviour is __consistent with the analyses__ that they act as a firewall—monitoring/protecting the Earth from unauthorized access.

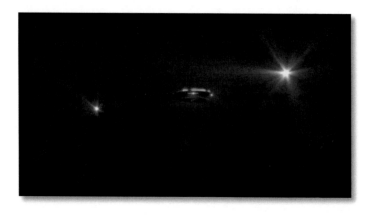

In 2016 – **a recent video of a SpaceX Falcon Rocket exploding** on the launch pad has raised eyebrows. The video stills indicated a "small silver sphere" flying over the rocket as it detonates. If this is the same sphere object as identified in this book, and the same sphere objects observed during WW2—this would mean these high speed airborne units are **weaponized** and have an array of **advanced countermeasure capabilities** designed specifically for aerial attack. Could this explain why these spheres suddenly turn up during large close-up UFO sightings / encounters and also why UFO's crash?, The reality is in order to bring down a high performance high technology aircraft - it would require a high technology weapon system.

Figure#17

Wednesday 19 December 2018

Location UK - Heathrow and Gatwick Airport are suddenly locked down due to a number of **low flying drones** over the airports... According to the BBC

- *Tens of thousands of passengers have been disrupted by drones flying over one of the UK's busiest airports.*

Gatwick's runway has been shut since Wednesday night, as devices have been repeatedly flying over the airfield. Sussex Police said it was not terror-related but a "deliberate act" of disruption, using "industrial specification" drones. About 110,000 passengers on 760 flights were due to fly on Thursday. Disruption could last "several days". An airline source told the BBC flights were currently cancelled until at least 19:00 GMT.

The airport advised that the runway would not open "until it was safe to do so". Defence Secretary Gavin Williamson has confirmed the Army has been called in to support Sussex Police. He said:

"The armed forces have a range of unique capabilities and this isn't something we would usually deploy but we are there to assist and do everything we can so that they are in a position to open the airport at the earliest opportunity." Those due to travel have been told to check the status of their flight, while Easyjet told its passengers not to go to Gatwick if their flights have been cancelled. The shutdown started just after 21:00 on Wednesday, when two drones were spotted flying "over the perimeter fence and into where the runway operates from". The runway briefly reopened at 03:01 on Thursday but was closed again about 45 minutes later amid "a further sighting of drones". The airport said at about 12:00 a drone had been spotted "in the last hour".

More than 20 police units from two forces are searching for the perpetrator, who could face up to five years in jail. Supt Justin Burtenshaw, head of armed policing for Sussex and Surrey, described attempts to catch whoever was controlling the drones as "painstaking" because it was "a difficult and challenging thing to locate them". "Each time we believe we get close to the operator, the drone disappears; when we look to reopen the airfield, the drone reappears," he said.

Reference: *https://www.theguardian.com/uk-news/2018/dec/19/gatwick-flights-halted-after-drone-sighting*

- *The army has been called in to help with the ongoing crisis at Gatwick airport, where drones flying near the runway have kept planes grounded for more than 24 hours. The airport has been closed since Wednesday night, when the devices were repeatedly flown over the airfield in what police and the airport described as a deliberate attempt to disrupt flights. Tens of thousands of travellers have been affected, with 110,000 passengers on 760 flights due to fly on Thursday. People camped out overnight at Gatwick, waiting for news of whether the airport would reopen on Friday. At around 9:30pm on Thursday Gatwick's chief operating officer Chris Woodroofe said the airport would be reviewing the situation overnight to see "whether there is any potential to open tomorrow" but they are "working up contingency plans all the way through to no flights tomorrow." Woodroofe said the situation remained "fluid", given the drone operator had not yet been found. He said the airport is expected to be closed for the "foreseeable future" while the hunt for the drone operator continues. The airport's advice is that those due to travel on Friday should check with their airline before arriving at the airport. The defence secretary, Gavin Williamson, told Sky News Sussex police had requested support from the armed forces. "We will be deploying the armed forces to give them the help that they need to be able to deal with the situation of the drones at Gatwick airport," he said. Williamson added that he could not say how the armed forces would help but said: "The armed forces have a range of unique capabilities and this isn't something we would usually deploy but we are there to assist and do everything we can so that they are in a position to open the airport at the earliest opportunity." Flights were suspended at Gatwick just after 9pm on Wednesday, when two drones were spotted flying near the runway. The runway briefly reopened at 03.01 on Thursday morning but closed 45 minutes later after a further drone sighting. There was another sighting around midday.*

With all that was going on the police had helicopters, sniffer dogs, and military assistance, however—they didn't intercept the drones, nor did they find/charge anyone. The oddest thing is the duration of the event—**the drones were reported to be hanging around for hours** while **Public domain** drones only **currently last 30 mins on a single charge.** In other words, these drones somehow **out-performed, out-matched, and outmanoeuvred** the UK armed forces and armed police for **hours.** It would appear these spheres observed as balls of light were trying to keep the planes on the ground for a period of time… **Was there something unwelcome in the local airspace that these spheres had to deal with?**

PART SEVENTEEN

LET'S TALK ABOUT MECHANISMS

If these spheres really are creating paranormal activity, how exactly could this be achieved? Let's work though some of the most commonly observed activities and see what we can find...

In close proximity, these spheres relay messages via a number of different broadcast mechanisms; EVP is the one of the most common.

The observable traits are as follows:

1) During EVP sessions the EVP playbacks can contain a number of different voices that each say separate words, these words are then sequenced into order creating one understandable sentence

2) The voices can sound quite different, with some using your own voice in an act of mimicking; while other voices are taken from environmental sources. This includes music, and other generic background sounds.

3) Strange clicking and / or pops are also present during the EVP playback. Technically, these audio issues can be interpreted as processing artefacts, these artefacts are formed as the sound wave is getting recreated / reconstructed / re-sequenced, hence errors occur and present themselves as pops / clicks

The fact that we observe different voices sequenced into one sentence means the AI system can't tell the difference between voice tones or area language. This has been a lingering question for years in the paranormal community-- investigators have long asked why a German ghost from the 18th century appears to speaks perfect English? It appears that the AI itself will identify the language used by the nearby person and match that language or it will just play back something random from its database that was recorded at an earlier time..

In the same way Animal Scientists may try to sequence basic animal language; they "may get it generally right" but not perfect. Likewise, the AI is trying to sequence human language, resulting in a generally correct content but the words/tone and locality may be very wrong...

By mimicking basic human interactions and speech patterns, the AI system pulls names from past observations stored within its database. Like all database technology, one needs to ask a specific question to get a specific answer, and this is what occurs during investigations—people ask who died here and they get a direct single name answer.

This technology isn't farfetched at all, as in 2018

Reference:

https://motherboard.vice.com/en_us/article/3k7mgn/baidu-deep-voice-software-can-clone-anyones-voice-with-just-37-seconds-of-audio

A new AI algorithm developed by Chinese tech giant Baidu can clone a pretty believable fake voice. The application *Deep Voice* can clone / model anyone's voice box with just 3.7 seconds of audio. As one can imagine this type of application brings many new national security risks, with the potential of cloning the voices of world leaders, and potentially triggering accidental conflict. Combine this Deep Voice application with AI and a dataset that is comparable to the current Google assistant or Amazon Alexia once can replicate EVP interactions. The question is how are they broadcast - with most only getting recorded on machines such as cameras or phones / tape recorders, while others are heard with the human ear? The answer is - they are getting transmitted in different ways.

First observed transmission mechanism - Audio broadcast via air, otherwise known as Direct Voice where EVP / Ghost voices can be heard with the human ear. The spheres identified in this book are using an exotic field based propulsion system, this system can create force on objects creating bangs and physical movement hence displaying the appearance of paranormal activity, if this field can create force on objects then there is no reason why it can't create force on the surrounding air

By resonating this field at high frequencies will create **compression and expansion** on the surrounding air resulting in audible sound waves a.k.a. voice(s). The side effect of this process appears to be the voice itself sounds **unnatural** / mechanical - and only a few words are produced in short bursts. **Figure #18**

Second observed transmission mechanism: Audio broadcast that's only picked up on electronic recording devices

- EVPs are broadcast from the sphere via directed electromagnetic radio waves into the unshielded circuit of a recorder; the circuit picks this up as **crosstalk.** Radio waves have the same effect on unshielded amplifiers. Human hearing **can't pick this up** as real-time human hearing is only based on sounds waves created via the compression and decompression (a.k.a. shaping of air).

Figure #19

However there is third observed mechanism which opens a whole new level of discussion

Example

A team is inside an active environment, the entirety of the experience is being recorded and live-streamed by mobile phones and cameras. On playback, the team can hear clear multiple EVPs; the EVPs are so loud that they echo around the room. Yet, although they are clear upon playback of <u>the recordings, no one on the team notices or hears the sound real-time.</u>

Fact one: If the sound/voice has an echo during playback, then the sound must be created by the compression/expansion of air, thus creating sound waves, which are then reflecting off the surrounding walls creating echo.

Figure #20

Sounds wave reflection

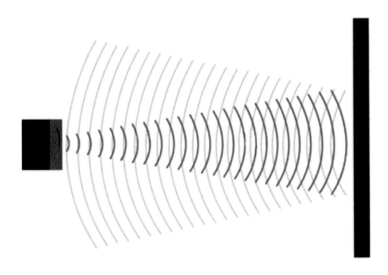

From observation: While the team cannot hear these voices real-time, people watching the experience online **can** hear these voices in real-time via live-stream. The audience alerts the team to the voices, but the team state they don't hear anything.

Fact two: according to https://www.hearinglink.org/your-hearing/about-hearing/how-the-ear-works/

*The sound waves are gathered by the outer **ear** and sent down the **ear** canal to the eardrum. The sound waves cause the eardrum to vibrate, which sets the three tiny bones in the middle **ear** into motion. The motion of the bones causes the fluid in the inner ear or cochlea to move.*

The anatomy of our hearing or auditory system is extremely complex but can be broadly divided into two parts, one being called 'peripheral' and the other 'central'.

- *The peripheral hearing system consists of three parts which are the outer ear, the middle ear and the inner ear:*
- *The outer ear consists of the pinna (also called the auricle), ear canal and eardrum.*
- *The middle ear is a small, air-filled space containing three tiny bones called the malleus, incus and stapes but collectively called the ossicles. The malleus connects to the eardrum linking it to the outer ear and the stapes (smallest bone in the body) connects to the inner ear.*
- *The inner ear has both hearing and balance organs. The hearing part of the inner ear and is called the cochlea which comes from the Greek word for 'snail' because of its distinctive coiled shape. The cochlea, which contains many thousands of sensory cells (called 'hair cells'), is connected to the central hearing system by the hearing or auditory nerve. The cochlea is filled with special fluids which are important to the process of hearing.*

The central hearing system consists of the auditory nerve and an incredibly complex pathway through the brain stem and onward to the auditory cortex of the brain.

In a nutshell, human hearing functions by the ear drum picking up vibrations in the air; in effect, sound waves then get converted to electrical impulses that travel onward into the auditory cortex of the brain for processing.

On the face of it, there is no reason why the group shouldn't be able to hear these sounds; however, there is one possible reason.

The human brain could be described as a transceiver—allowing it to receive and transmit information to and from an external source.

As mentioned these spheres use a field-based propulsion system; to create sound - these spheres would need to resonate the propulsion field creating force on the surrounding air. This force compresses and expands the air to create sound waves. These waves **enter** the human ear and are thereby converted into nerve impulses and directed into the auditory cortex.

To prevent this reception of sound waves, and ultimately block the brain from receiving auditory information from the nerves, requires a process / or subject area - scientists are only beginning to tap into.

The only way the sound waves generated by the spheres can be blocked from processing by an unimpeded human ear is by a digital intercept on the neural level. To effectively achieve a complete blockage, the sphere would need to perform a local electronic intercept signal alongside the (otherwise audible by the human ear) audio signal.

One way this could be possible, is if the sphere can simultaneously transmit commands directly into the temporal lobe of the listeners in immediate proximity, thereby blocking incoming auditory data in real-time but permitting auditory data processing upon playback of a recording, while those listening via live stream won't be affected and will be able to hear the sounds clearly.

Processing sensory input of the temporal lobe in detail

Auditory

Adjacent areas in the superior, posterior, and lateral parts of the temporal lobes are involved in high-level auditory processing. The temporal lobe is involved in primary auditory perception, such as hearing, and holds the primary auditory cortex.

The primary auditory cortex receives sensory information from the ears and secondary areas process the information into meaningful units such as speech and words.

The superior temporal gyrus includes an area (within the lateral fissure) where auditory signals from the cochlea first reach the cerebral cortex and are processed by the primary auditory cortex in the left temporal lobe.

Like all systems—if it's possible for a sphere to transmit commands directly into a human temporal lobe for the purposes of blocking real-time hearing, the overall capacity of a sphere and ensuing implications will reach far beyond simply intercepting auditory data.

This would imply that not only can these spheres externally **insert and block** incoming auditory nerve impulses, but the spheres could impact the **visual processing function of the human frontal lobe.**

Visual

The areas associated with vision in the temporal lobe interpret the meaning of visual stimuli and establish object recognition.[citation needed] The ventral part of the temporal cortices appear to be in-

volved in high-level visual processing of complex stimuli such as faces (fusiform gyrus) and scenes (parahippocampal gyrus). Anterior parts of this ventral stream for visual processing are involved in object perception and recognition.

Therefore, we can conclude that it's **very likely** that these spheres can also directly broadcast **visions** to a human target(s) or perform advanced masking techniques. Employing a masking technique implies that the sphere could appear to the human as another entity entirely, such as a adult or child or perceived angels & demons.

The question begs: Could the spheres' audio-visual manipulation of the human experience be the mechanism that influenced the founding of many world religions? Consider the following examples from the New American Standard Bible.

Daniel 10:7

Now I, Daniel, alone saw the vision, while the men who were with me did not see the vision; nevertheless, a great dread fell on them, and they ran away to hide themselves.

Acts 18:9

And the Lord said to Paul in the night by a vision, "Do not be afraid any longer, but go on speaking and do not be silent

Acts 12:9

And he went out and continued to follow, and he did not know that what was being done by the angel was real, but thought he was seeing a vision

Genesis 15:1

After these things the word of the LORD came to Abram in a vision, saying, "Do not fear, Abram, I am a shield to you; Your reward shall be very great."

Acts 9:10

Now there was a disciple at Damascus named Ananias; and the Lord said to him in a vision, "Ananias." And he said, "Here I am, Lord

What we call poltergeists sometimes show incredible intelligence and abilities, at 30 East Drive for instance its common that people see a plastic lemon appear in mid air and fly across the room, other times playing cards are stacked up in triangles in a blink of an eye. However at other times, investigators observe the total opposite; limited or absence of ability coupled with relatively mindless foolishness. This abrupt change in behaviour may indicate a switch between rule-based AI and remote access AI. As mentioned these spheres operate in two modes—with the near to ground based network operating in Active mode—meaning they are up linking and sending signals between each other and the passive spheres in the area. While the passive spheres that are roaming around monitoring/protecting/extracting from areas of genetic interest.

What do I call rule-based AI?

Rule-based Artificial intelligence engages when **certain observations or actions** are made by the sphere resulting in a pre- programmed **default behaviour or response.**

Rule-based AI can explain why paranormal activity references the same action types (or default behaviours/ responses to a certain stimuli) worldwide:

- Objects thrown about
- Scratching/banging
- Limited communication via EVP or audio
- Image projection
- Mathematical demonstrations, such as household items suddenly arranging themselves in mathematical order.

What do I call remote access AI?

In the I.T. world, remote access is a critical part of our everyday work. Remote access is when an operator or engineer can connect to a server anywhere in the world and take control of the machine. Likewise, an airborne drone is controlled from a location outside of the drone itself (such as a nearby human being with a remote control). Therefore, it is totally possible for **someone (or something) to remotely access** a smaller more advanced airborne drone system such as a sphere. During a remote access connection, the drone would be performing much more advanced **interactions** than the normal rule-base AI actions.

Speculation: It would appear these spheres are employing a form of quantum mechanics. If this is true, it may be possible that spheres can operate as a bridge between their current location and another point in space. Paranormal researchers call this bridge a Portal where spirits can enter this world. If my analysis is correct then these "spirits" are not dead people but are in fact "different groups of extra terrestrials" that are discreetly getting inserted and extracted from the Earth, staying out of general view by using a stealth technology that allows them to hide in the light but never the less can be seen up close by IR / Full spectrum cameras it would mean there is a good chance there is already a heavy extra terrestrial presence on Earth that's operating outside of the human race's perceptive ability.

Summary of silver sphere capabilities

- There are two distinct and mutually exclusive behaviours that spheres engage in. This allows us to classify spheres into one of two types; 1) passive; or 2) active.

Passive spheres: operational behaviour is mostly observational; in areas of genetic interest passive spheres are monitoring, engaging is resource protection when necessary, and/or extracting DNA; passive spheres also communicate to the weaponized firewall sphere clusters by performing low level airspace monitoring and controlling access to resources.

Active spheres: operational behaviour is designated to key areas; These active spheres primary task is to create a low to ground wireless network using burst transmission protocols (which the passive spheres and weaponized firewall spheres uplink to); active spheres will use electronic and physical countermeasures to keep humans at a safe distance from high frequency broadcast emissions.

- **Autonomous rule-based AI** observation system, when in close proximity it mimics basic human interaction by a small range of broadcast mechanisms

- **System management** - Line of sight control—top down control from a geo-sync platform following the 11pm to 3am time period.

- **State Change**—allowing the solid sphere object to pass though other solid objects such as walls as observed during WW2 - known as Quantum Tunnelling

- Coated in **Metamaterial** converting visible light to different wavelengths/deep IR rendering it near invisible to the human eye yet visible to specialist cameras and some animals also can create a super black appearance.

- Able to create a **black masking** effect—allowing active/adaptive camouflage within low light environments

- **Propulsion system** anti-gravity type with a static field by-product - the same system can create force and use small objects as projectiles (such as marbles) this artificially created force could also have a radioactive by-product which can imprint on physical materials such as stone or wood emitting a form of (currently undetectable) low level radiation that has a negative impact on human health.

- **Atomic 3D Projection**—where data can be converted into physical matter for a short period, during this time the projection is as solid as a normal object. This sounds farfetched but recently scientists have found a process to convert light into matter

Reference
http://www3.imperial.ac.uk/newsandeventspggrp/imperialcolle
ge/newssummary/news_16-5-2014-15-32-44

- **Electromagnetic signal transmission**—this mechanism is used to broadcast signals which interact with the human/animal nervous system making the receptor feel uneasy sick or nervous, this could be used as a **non lethal** weapon to keep unwanted attention at bay. During this broadcast it has been observed that animals including insects within the local area suddenly go silent. Same capability can perform directed radio broadcasts on to physical devices such as radios/picked up as crosstalk—overriding the external signal including static delivering simple direct responses.

- **EVP—Two observed mechanisms**—One AI (artificial intelligence) based—Real-time processing and broadcasting of sentences constructed by **captured** audio samples mixed together to create a message, three or four different voices can be heard in the same sentence - these finish with a **pop** or an **click** these have been observed to generally repeat. This pop and clicking issue is a digital process artefact caused by errors within the encoding/sequencing process.

- The other is **Remote Access** operates the same as any communication device where someone on the line—EVPs are broadcast from the sphere via electromagnetic waves directed into the electronics of a recorder—the circuit picks it up as **crosstalk** the same process as radio waves on a unshielded amplifier. Human hearing can't pick this up as we use the compression and decompression of air.

- **Audio broadcast via air**—by using the propulsion system air can be **compressed and expanded at high frequency** to create a noise or a voice, the side effect of this process is that the sound **sounds** digital and fuzzy/hollow and only a few word can be produced. The same process of using the propulsion system can create **force** allows it to bang rapidly on objects.

- **Possession**—the human brain is a computer and like all computers it has an operating system, Operating systems have security flaws that can allow **remote access**—remote access is perceived on a human level as "**possession**", The human brain is also a transceiver meaning it broadcasts and receives signals—a signal is locally broadcast from these objects exploiting genetic security flaws, taking control of the hosts actions

- **Electromagnetic Jamming**—knocking out cameras and phones via a high frequency EM pulse (observed at 30 East Drive and other locations)

- **Masking**—Can emit a signal into the temporal lobe visual cortex that makes the receptor hallucinate; can be used on tight groups of people which share the same hallucination—again exploiting genetic security flaws, this is why many people report to see a ghost but the cameras see a glowing orb which is the silver sphere object in a quantum state. allowing an array of masking and communication capabilities

- **Dual mode control** - During Rule-base AI control - The same door will bang the same words will be heard—same actions replicate - this is the AI in action. During Remote Access— more intelligent interactions occur

- **Rule based AI passive observation system utilizing quantum mechanics**—line of sight control—automated to observe general area (**countrywide**) and areas of genetic resource.

- Trigger based logic meaning a **set of events**/or **technical signatures** which gains its attention **See test later in the book**—otherwise known as parameters

- **Genetic sampling—observed as three parallel scratches / cuts on skin, in effect micro biopsy skin cell and blood sampling**

- **Weapon capable**, Use of very high energy directed XRAY / Gamma ray radiation, used for interception of unauthorised crafts, enforcing airspace control, capable of electronically disrupting and causing destruction of aircraft and objects

PART EIGHTEEN

DISTURBING BEHAVIOURS

What about Scratching?

The patterns and behaviour of paranormal activity indicates that it is a front for protecting the sphere's access to a valuable resource—earth's genetic material. It would seem that when a person flags (or triggers) the spheres too much the sphere in closest proximity will perform an aggressive act and scratch the perpetrator.

But what is the physical evidence of this?

Observe the betz sphere below: notice the triangle in the lower quadrant of the sphere, and the corresponding three edges. The sphere will **scuff** the human aggressor, always resulting in three long straight scratch lines. This is why the scratch marks or cuts follow the **same path and distance** as the scratches curves.

Figure #21

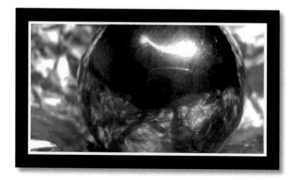

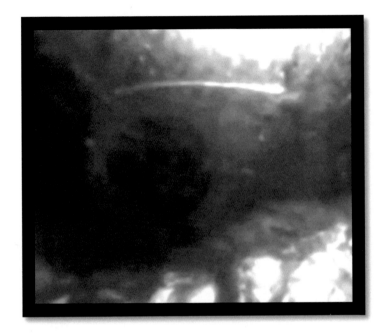

Figure #22

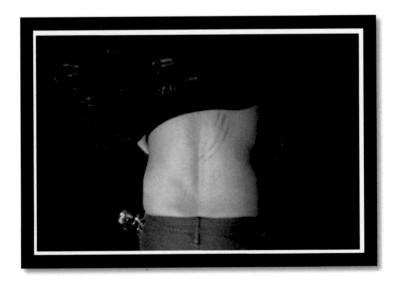

When people are scratched they report feeling a burning sensation, this is consistent with a heat or electrical burn.

This action signifies skin & blood DNA sampling, however while is often perceived as a demonic spirit in the eyes of the paranormal community. The reality is, scratching is just an action to push people away. It's the equivalent of aggressively pulling a pet out of the way of impending danger.

Figure#23

However, there is another more disturbing behaviour observed.

Figure #24 is the missing person's map of the US national parks service. Groups of people have vanished **and the few** that are located have been found dead on remote mountain tops.

This is a **full extraction process** which would need to be performed by a **craft much larger than a sphere.** The extraction process is not only often fatal, but any bodily remains may be mutilated. This is not a passive **DNA extraction** process as described as above, but an **aggressive action**. This behaviour pattern change suggests that a second group is responsible for these full extractions and/or mutilations.

Figure #24

Above is a map of strange disappearances in US national parks, are these missing people getting extracted? Or simply getting lost, trapped in some of the approx 5000 caves? Without full access to a clean dataset it's hard to say.

The following images are from human and cattle mutilations appear to have the same types of incisions and injuries. Note the jaw and eye extraction with surgical precision; as the injury's pattern match, it suggests the same process is used - meaning the same group is responsible.

Reference: *http://www.alienvideo.net/0805/alien-abduction-mutilation.php*

From the Autopsy Report:

"*The auxiliary regions on both sides showed soft spots where organs had been removed. Incisions were made on the face, internal thorax, abdomen, legs, arms, and chest. Shoulders and arms have perforations of 1 to 1.5 inches in diameter where tissue and muscles were extracted. The edges of the perforations were uniform and so was their size. The chest had shrunk due to the removal of internal organs., We observed the removal of the right and left orbital areas, emptying of the mouth cavity, pharynx, oropharynx, neck, right and left armpit area, abdomen, pelvic cavity, right and left groin area*". Precise "*cookie cutter*" holes are discovered in strategical positions throughout the body used for extracting internal organs. This level of precision suggests that the operation was executed with speed, the application of heat or lasers, all occurring as the subject was still alive.*

(cause of the death): .acute haemorrhage in multiple traumatisms. There is a component of causa mortis by vagus stimulation" (implying cardio-respiratory arrest caused by extreme pain). "*The victim shows injuries with vital reaction characteristics, i.e., there is the component "torture". The suggested modus operandi is: incisions in soft parts and natural orifices using sucking devices*".

Figure #25

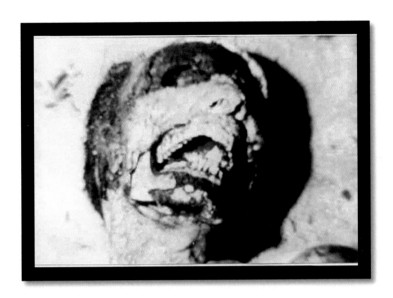

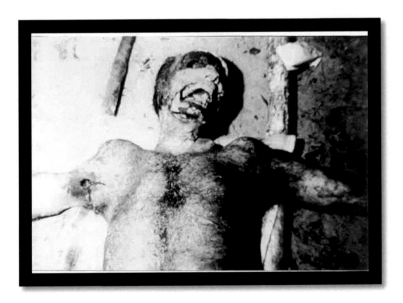

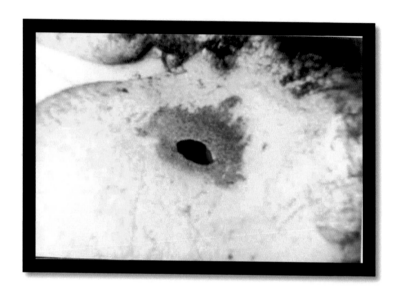

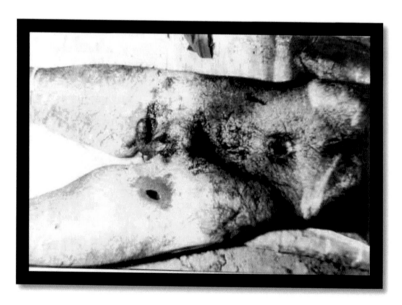

Figure #26

It is clear that this is a **totally different behaviour pattern**, meaning it's a **totally different group, with an entirely different agenda**. The logic of the above injuries is to extract as much cellular DNA as possible in the **shortest period of time, in other words the injuries indicates a "get in and get out quick" behaviour.**

Full extraction and/or mutilation injuries indicate: 1)a pipe or machine is punched through the skin; 2) a chemical agent, possibly ammonia type acid is inserted; 3) the chemical agent converts the inner organs to a liquid cellular state; 4) rapid extraction of blood and now liquified internal organs though high-powered suction. This process is rapid and brutal; from the expressions observed on the victims faces, this process is done so fast the victims simply don't have the time to die, the existing oxygen levels in the brain indicate victims are semi-conscious though the whole event, and will later expire from their injuries.

So, what does all this mean?

We have two observable processes at work; the first sphere-based process is a passive observation and genetic monitoring/protection/extraction system. Sphere initiated extractions are performed on the quiet; the sphere network will masks itself under the shroud of ghosts or paranormal activity. The source of the second observable process is not the work of spheres, and is instead a **brutal hit and run technique.**

These two different **behaviours** indicate that one **is protective of human life** and the other is not.

Could this be what the late Boyd Bushman was referring to?

* According to Bushman, the defence industry put extra-terrestrials into two groups and nickname them "The Rustlers" and "The Wranglers."
* The Wranglers are providing assistance (sphere-based AI) while the Rustlers "just take" (full-extraction/ mutilation based behaviour / actions)

The sphere's observation system firewall component are the guards (Wranglers) trying to keep the Rustlers out. Like all forces, the sphere network has its limitations, and **now and again** the Rustlers manage to get through this security and perform hit and run style actions to a select number of earth's biological life forms.

Follow the logic and connections with naturally fall into place

"The Lord has eyes everywhere looking for good and evil"

http://biblehub.com/proverbs/15-3.htm

This quote from the Bible could be cryptic description of a surveillance/monitoring/protection system that is watching over us. As all systems like this, they **need to be automated** and they have logic **of behaviour.**

Over the years NASA live-streams have accidentally shown massive spacecrafts have come close to the orbiting ISS (international space station). The crafts are clearly technically superior but shows to have no interest in engaging, but rather get away as fast as they can... **the question is why?**

The only logical conclusion is there is a greater force controlling access to the Earth and orders other external groups to leave. From this, I argue that the Earth is a **controlled airspace,** or more specifically, the Earth is in **an involuntary state of isolated seclusion.**

Figure #27 the ISS livecam

Reference: *https://www.youtube.com/watch?v=MGfzMdDxijM*

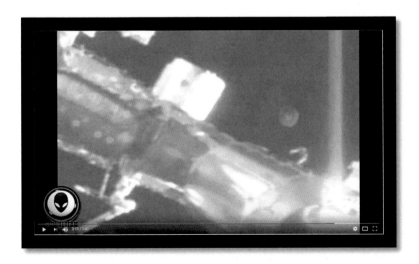

#Figure #28 – Close up

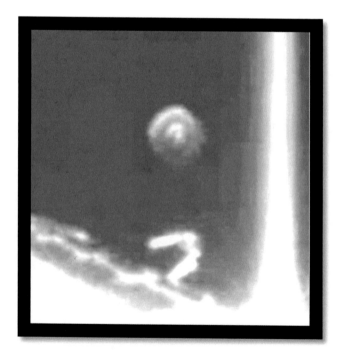

PART NINETEEN

HOW TO TRIGGER THE AI SPHERE OBSERVATION SYSTEM (PARANORMAL ACTIVITY)

The best example to explain the behaviour of this observation system - is that of an AI application currently getting used in our everyday banking system, This application is called AML transaction Monitoring. (Anti Money Laundering transaction Monitoring)

- *Anti-money laundering (AML) transaction monitoring software allows banks and other financial institutions to monitor customer transactions on a daily basis or in real-time for risk. ... The transactions monitored can include cash deposits and withdrawals, wire transfers, and ACH activity.*

The AML system monitors in real-time the spending / transaction patterns of clients and companies,

Behind this application there is a database, that database is where all the data is kept, this is generally either Microsoft SQL based or Oracle (Oracle Corporation). By monitoring the spending patterns over a period of time the application can create an overall spending model where old records can be referenced with new, when transactions are requested that are outside of the normal pattern, this transaction is flagged up for staff or security to review.

There are two ways anomalous transactions are flagged: 1) by SQL/Oracle database datasets with reports (Real-time Business intelligence BIDS) running against them; or 2) the more advanced AI solutions which can block and trace in real-time.

The system of automated databases/datasets and reporting is the foundation of current intelligence gathering/analytical systems used by intelligence agencies around the world, and this external observation system is no different. Just as this AML system looks for out-of-place transactional anomalies this external observation system is also looking for out-of-place anomalies, all I needed to do was figure out what anomalies it is looking for...

> *"Satan himself keeps transforming himself into an angel of light."—2 Corinthians 11:14.*

So let's think about this... we know the drone-type silver sphere observation system would need to be automated to monitor on such a massive scale. Automation means that spheres would need to be **autonomous** (to be able to make its own decisions in real-time). These real-time decisions are made based on a set of pre-coded rules; this coding is what I describe as rule-based artificial intelligence. Meaning when certain environmental observations are acquired, a pre-determined action is executed

Reports of small silver spheres are commonly observed during large UFO events / encounters, these repetitive observations are an outlier to the typical sphere behaviour. I wondered if these larger UFO crafts were "the anomalies" this observation system was looking out for – and once discovered - results in a pre-determined action. This would mean these spheres are not part of the larger UFO but in fact- engaging the UFO. So the question is what could this trigger be?

On observation these UFOs are appear to be using field-based propulsion. When a high enough energy source interacts with a gaseous atmosphere of **oxygen and nitrogen,** the gas molecules will emits photons. This is exactly the same interaction mechanism that creates the **light** during electrical storms. As a result these objects will emit a very high concentration of natural pure light - for example like that of a pure electric blue

Credit: *https://weheartit.com/entry/257475576*

Figure #29

UFO sighting: Las Vegas mystery as Christmas UFO stuns party city

Reference: *https://www.express.co.uk/news/weird/1221270/UFO-news-aliens-Christmas-sighting-update-latest-las-vegas-Nevada*

- *A UFO sighting in Nevada has stunned a paranormal enthusiast as a bright light hovered over Las Vegas and appeared to zoom in various directions over the hills. A UFO sighting in Las Vegas has confused onlookers as the bright orb moved quickly along the hillside while emitting pulsating bright white and blue lights. The man recording the video claimed that the UFO covered an estimated 50 miles in three minutes and was recorded days before Christmas on December 19. This apparent distance travelled would mean the UFO was moving at speeds around 1,000 miles an hour, only slighter slower than a F-35 stealth aircraft*

Figure 30#

If the Earth is being kept in a state of seclusion, and the (type one) spheres are acting as a firewall, then the most likely trigger of would be that of **light signatures**. In the same way the banking AML monitoring works by tracking transactions patterns—this system would operate by tracking light patterns. So, in order to attract the attention of these spheres I need to replicate this light signature in an **out-of-place** area to trigger the **rule-based AI** into action.

Out-of-Place area is the term I am using to refer to an area with limited light emissions. Areas such as busy roads wouldn't work, as the constant movement of headlights would be filtered out and ignored by this system. This baseline light is what's called a Noise Gate/Threshold.

I went to a visit a friend in Sutton London; the area was very quiet, and with next to no light pollution it was pitch back. It was here I did my first of three tests. I placed a number of small LED strobes in a reflective container with relatively small diameter. This created a small but very concentrated vertical light source that was in a state of flux. Then I placed three vertical static detectors around the LED light source I had constructed.

- **State of flux**—the test light source had no constant light signature, and instead was a dynamic, random, and anomalous noisy emission.

By only emitting **vertical light,** whatever that might be detected or **starts interacting** with the sensors has to be in the **line of sight** (as in **directly above** the test source.)

By doing this, I am 1) under the assumption that the Earth is in seclusion; and 2) one of the system **triggers** is **looking for unauthorised craft or objects.** I figured that my light signature (**although not perfect)** might be enough to trigger the system in to action. I started the test at 11pm in total darkness—within **45 seconds** of the vertical LED strobe getting switched on, the detectors lit up and tracked an energy source that was emitting a vertical static field—exactly the same electrical behaviour as observed in haunted houses. Below my Mark1 unit, a vertical light emitter surrounded by static Field detectors

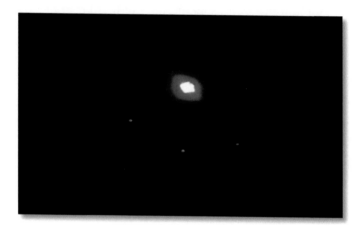

Figure #31

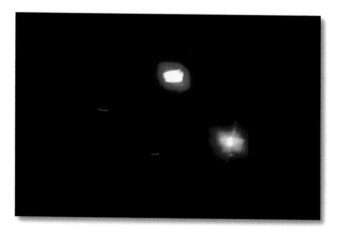

Conclusion: The observation system has come into range and the **rule-based AI** is triggered by the **out-of-place** light signature that is similar to a (UFO) electrical field-based population craft.

- I theorise - The vertical static detectors are picking up the **static by-product** of the type 1 (firewall) sphere's **propulsion system** as it drops down and flies across to take a closer look at the light source.

Test Two: Manchester, UK

To double down on my theory, I went to the extreme. I decided to re-run the test in Manchester UK at 11:00pm; but this time it was on top of a hill; approx 3,000 feet up; well away from any electrical interference. I came up with a stronger and more focused version of the LED strobe and my friend Michael Postlethwaite came along to film it, the same "Mike" who was my cameraman for the tests at 30 East Drive. Mike did some electronics work and had built a number of static field detectors—my plan was to run all of these static detectors together and see if they trigger at the same time. Little did I know - that the outcome of this test would be set in my mind forever...

Figure #32

Below: Mark 2 unit. Vertical concentrated light emitter, surrounded by vertical static detectors

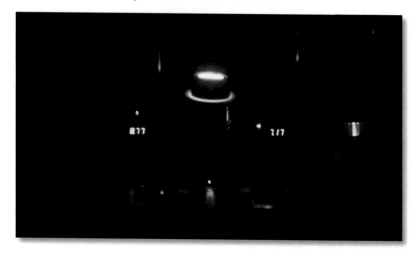

Test was performed on the hills located near Woodhead tunnel Manchester

Figure #33

After one hour of waiting around, suddenly it all came to life. **Both the vertical static field detectors** and **Mike's audio alerting static detectors started tracking** an **artifical signal**. Below is the audio extract. Notice the consistent levels—this is an **artificial signal which is demonstrating high frequency pulsing**, a very possible behaviour of a field-based propulsion system.

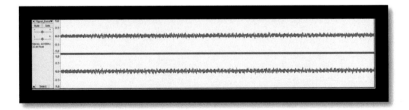

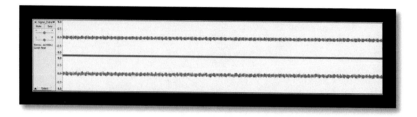

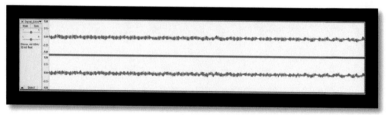

The wave forms above appear to be presenting high frequency pulsing from a source that was moving closer then moving away. creating the dopper effect; while the source was moving around us, a number of EVPs were silmuntaneously recorded appearing to voice mimick. At one point, Mike mentioned that he felt spooked— and on the recording - a voice matching mine says, *"feel spooked?"* just at the point I talk over it. This is an example of AI voice cloning, but also other effects occurred such as visual experiences with myself and mike physically seening shadows of what looked to be people watching us. Test 2 was a success: my out-of-place concentrated light source triggered the external AI monitoring system, pushing the spheres into action, the pre-programmed response was executed = resulted in attempted interception. Once the sphere arrived, clearly no craft but something "unidentified", the sphere then monitored it, and escalated the case to a higher level. It would appear that this higher level consists of living beings that get temporarily inserted to observe whats going on.

Figure #34

Below - Mike totally blown away as he reviews the recording

Test Three

I decided to push my theory further. Mike and I designed and built a unit specify designed to trigger the AI monitoring system into action; in other words, trigger paranormal activity on demand.

This operated on the same principles as in the Mark 2 unit by creating a concentrated light source using a colour that mimics electrical gas interaction. Also to increase the chances of it working I used a glass sphere to defuse the light.

By all accounts, this glowing sphere of concentrated light would trick this AI monitoring system into thinking an unauthorized craft has entered controlled airspace as from directly above this unit mimics a craft using field-based propulsion, The following photos tell their own story...

Mark 3 unit as seen from above

Figure #35

Mark 3 unit side / front view

Figure #36

Figure #37

Reaction

Figure #38

Vertical Static fields detected on-demand.

Figure #39

Figure#40

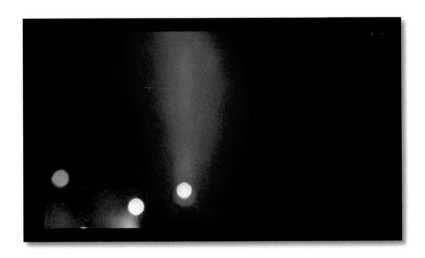

Figure #41

As this was recorded an EVP came over

"We are the Anomaly"

I personally have no idea what Figure #40 could be, however the description of the Peruvian skull found in Peru matches the appearance of the one presented above.

Reference: https://www.express.co.uk/news/weird/918241/Aliens-UFO-Paracas-skulls-DNA-tests-Peru-Brian-Foerster

ALIEN SKULLS? Shock verdict after DNA tests reveal where 'elongated heads came from'

DNA test results on the elongated skulls discovered in Peru have been released by a researcher investigating if the bones could belong to an alien race. The 3,000-year old Paracas skulls, with elongated craniums, have long been held up by UFO hunters as evidence of ancient alien visitations due to their extraordinarily huge foreheads. Researcher Brian Foerster initally thought the discovery would not fit into the "known evolutionary tree". The Paracas skulls were discovered on the desert peninsula of Paracas, on the southern coast of Peru, by native archaeologist Julio Tello in 1928. In 2015, discussing earlier DNA tests on the remains, he said: "The mitochondrial DNA (from the mother) presented mutations unknown to any man, primate or any other animal and the mutations suggested we are dealing with a completely new human-like being, very distant from Homo sapiens, Neanderthals or Denisovans.

"I am not sure it will even fit into the known evolutionary tree."

Research by sceptics later uncovered that those involved had a history of involvement and belief in research into paranormal subjects such as the Yeti and so-called alien hybrids, an alleged cross breed between humans and aliens. Now Mr Foerster, who is director of the Paracas History Museum, has released details of DNA tests he said were carried out in conjunction with the Peruvian Government and he appears to now accept they were probably human in origin.

In two video updates about the DNA, Mr Foerster made no mention of extraterrestrials. He described how the Paracas skulls appeared to share DNA links with other elongated skulls found between the Black Sea and the Caspian Sea.

Mr Foerster believes the elongation is not just caused by artificial cranial deformation, but rather by genetics with some of the elongated skulls cranial volume being up to 25 per cent larger and 60 per cent heavier than conventional human skulls.

He says this means that they could not have been intentionally deformed through head binding or flattening, as cranial deformation can change the shape but does not alter the volume or weight of a skull.

Speaking at the Elongated Skulls Symposium in Los Angeles, Mr Foerster said: "What it does show for sure is that the Paracas elongated skull people were not 100 per cent Native American.

"They were a mix or even you could say, in some ways, a hybrid of different people".

"Their blood types are very complicated as well, they should be blood type O if they're 100 percent Native American and that's not the case"

"We are likely looking at a sub-species of humanity as regards to the Paracas. It seems to be a lot of DNA evidence from extreme Eastern Europe and extreme western Asia"

"More specifically I'm talking about the area in between the Black Sea and the Caspian Sea where ancient elongated skull people lived I think about 3,000 years ago"

"So I think we are looking at a migration pattern starting in the Caspian Black Sea area and then entering through the Persian Gulf and then moving eastwards eventually winding up on the coast of Peru."

He added: *"It appears that the largest elongated skulls on the planet have been found, A in Paracas, Peru and B in the Caucasus area in between the Black Sea and the Caspian Sea".*

"So my theory is that there was a sub-species of human which we are going to be eventually calling Homo-Sapiens-Sapiens-Paracas, and they were living in the area in between the Caspian and Black Sea."

"They were invaded by somebody and so they were forced to flee."

Archaeologist Mr Tello found more than 300 of the odd skeletal remains in a complex grave system in 1928.

Does this skull below look like the face in the image? You decide...

Figure #42

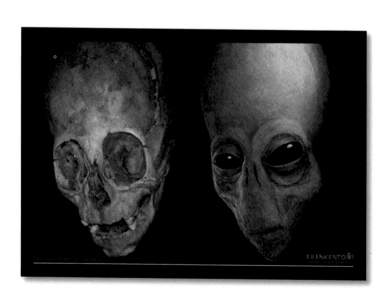

Part Twenty

A GLIMPSE INTO PANDORA'S BOX

If we are under the assumption that the earth is in a state of seclusion, that would mean that the airspace / physical- monitoring/DNA resource-monitoring/passive extraction/sampling/actions are all performed by the same sphere system

But the aggressive **hit-and-run** extractions are *not*—hence the need for **rapid** action.

- If this is the case, that would indicate there is a conflict or war between two rival groups.
- As my tests demonstrated, one of the sphere's triggers is the observation of unauthorised crafts or objects. This has been validated by other reports of witnesses seeing the same sphere objects in close proximity to a larger UFO craft. This same behaviour pattern was observed during WW2 with the air force on both the allied and the axis powers experiencing close encounters with these small sphere objects.
- It appears these firewall spheres are weaponised—upon identification of an earthly / unearthly craft, a friend or foe decision is made.
- This implies that UFOs *don't crash* but are intercepted; this sphere system acts as a firewall between us and a negative external group. First identified by Boyd Bushman as "the Rustlers", it appears that these objects do their best to protect the earth and its DNA resources, but as with all forces, it is limited in numbers—therefore now and again it logical that this negative force will - on occasion slip though the net and

negative events will occur.

At this point it would seem that **the paranormal** has been totally **misinterpreted.** Paranormal activity appears to be the result of an **artificial system managed by Rule-based A.I.**; the spheres shroud behind advanced masking capabilities and/or directly interacting with the human temporal lobe.

If my analysis is correct, logically the genetic material samples maybe used as reference data for possible upgrade work and deployments on the human race. However, while the collection of genetic material is one endeavour, the successful transport of genetic material is entirely another. The latter is not only difficult, but would require huge storage areas equipped with cryogenic containers suitable for possible long trips.

Unless, of course... the labs receiving samples from this sphere system are much closer than we think? To perform the fleet of genetic testing and deployments on 7.6 billion people would require a huge work force consisting of massive labs, research areas, and would need to be local enough for extraction, deployments, and storage. NASA , flew an aging satellite into the surface of the moon and it was reported they had a surprise—"the moon rang like a bell" *for almost an hour.* The only way this ringing can be explained, is if the moon itself is a hollowed out sphere. In other words, the moon was formed through artificial means.

Satellite images of the moon have spotted something interesting.

Each one of the small rectangles in Figure # is 1KM long. The white reflection on the rectangles is what looks to be *flat roofs.* Could this area be an artificial construct that's located on the bottom side of the moon?

Figure #43

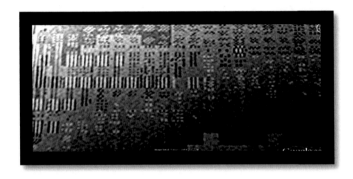

Figure # is just one small section of a massive area.

Figure #44

- Just one of these vertical-like disks is 5KM thick at its thickest point and 30KM long.
- Logic suggests that this infrastructure is **suitable for mass**

genetic work and mass storage.

SPECULATION

- According to the late researcher Lloyd Pye, book: *Everything You Know Is Wrong: Human Origins*, there is a **genetic bridge** between primates and another DNA type. This bridge indicates that humans are a **product of artificial genetic fusion** done by artificially engineering x2 the data into one chromosome. As a result of this **cut-and-paste** we have thousands of genetic defects causing cancers and degenerative diseases.

- It would appear the human race was a technical project that started well didn't complete, did something occur that halted work?

Figure# 45

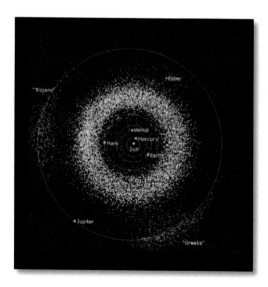

Revelation 12:7-17 - New international version

Then war broke out in heaven. Michael and his angels fought against the dragon, and the dragon and his angels fought back

The above reference to **heaven** could be a misinterpretation of the word **Space.** Meaning, there was a **war in space** between two rival groups (the angels and the dragon).

The locations of these massive asteroid belts **could be** the signature of shattered and destroyed planets; this would suggest that the earth and its people are the last survivors of a **biblical war** in space.

Figure #46

This is NASA's simulated image of Planet earth with all of the water removed;

it would seem it too was attacked destroying a huge chunk of its upper crust.

On February 7th 2020, an interesting NASA livestream occurred that was sourced from the onboard ISS camera. On the face of it, the video shows what appears to be **space craft's** engaging **other space crafts** and having what could be described a **"biblical battle in heaven?"**

War in heaven? or space?

Dragon or Spaceship?

Figure #47 – Filmed from the ISS LiveCam 1 of 3

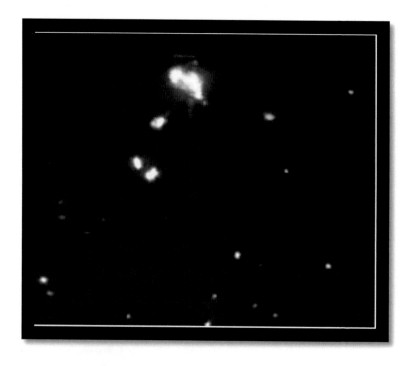

Figure #48 Filmed from the ISS LiveCam 2 of 3

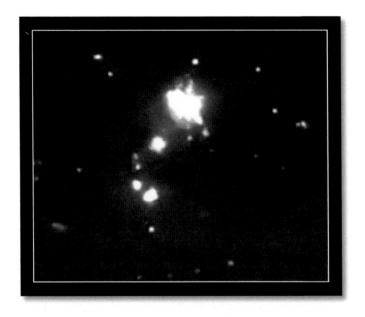

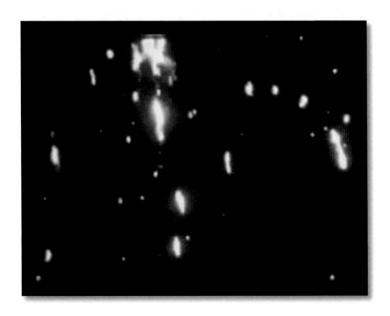

Final conclusion

I theorise that as Boyd Bushman stated,

"There are two groups"

"The "Rustlers" and "The Wranglers"

With one group having deployed a **planetary wide Quantum-Based Observation System and Weapons Platform**, This platform is designed to control Earth's airspace, acting as a benevolent firewall between the human race and malicious external groups and their interests. This firewall controls what can leave and what can enter planet earth's atmosphere, whereby the spheres will intercept unauthorised vehicles.

From observation there appears to be three the types of configurations - Type A (Firewall) — Type B (Environmental) and Type C (Hard Node)

The first Type A **"firewall clusters"** operating at approx 100.000 ft seen in long lines or clusters.

The firewall sphere clusters are weaponized, they control access to our local airspace and space itself, controlling what enters and leaves.

They connect to the ground network using directed burst transmission protocols, once data has been sent - the ground network (hard nodes) then allows long distance encrypted data relay with low probability of detection or interception.

This mechanism prevents **real-time** location data of the high altitude units, as the signal is directed downwards and can't be picked up and cross correlated. In many respects it's similar to our Military Satellites operating in orbit, but instead of using space they relay from the ground.

The second are Type B **"Environmental spheres"** that monitor areas of generic interest.

Environmental spheres appear to operate low to the ground, these are generally passive and slow moving, appear to use (as Bob Lazar terms) omicron mode for flight. This mode is said to unstable during slow speeds and bad weather. During heavy rain and thunder they appear these spheres shelter in tunnels or caves. During that time people within these tunnels will experience paranormal like activity. These appear to operate in areas of rich genetic resource be that natural woodland areas or areas with high concentration of humans DNA.

And third - are the Type C **"Hard Node"** spheres that operate in perceived haunted houses; these operate as the underlining communication architecture.

The hard nodes appear to be operating as a network relay using burst transmissions, they operate in one of two places, one the **top of the building or the basement**, they **deploy two smaller spheres approx the size of cricket balls** - these monitor different areas and operate as one cluster, in effect a MASTER / SLAVE0 / SLAVE1 configuration.

This is why multiple paranormal events can occur at one time around the same building, as these spheres are operating as one - and can execute commands simultaneously.

The closer one gets to the broadcasting sphere the more aggressive paranormal like activity will occur, as thus forcing / creating space between the source and persons... High freq microwave broadcasts and by-products from its propulsion system appear to emit a form of radiation poisoning resulting in localised sickness and headaches & overtime - possible mental illness.

By using the field-based propulsion system it creates force on objects/impacts - banging on walls doors / footsteps and other physical effect while at the same time - using other electronic countermeasures that disrupt the human nervous system creating negative physical effects. These countermeasures could be defined as Non-Lethal designed **to create space** between the transmission area and the person = **the inverse-square law** states that just doubling the distance from a **source of radiation reduces radiation intensity by 75%**. Hence people are chased from rooms but not buildings allowing the broadcast to occur safety

This hard node network is in effect small spheres using artificial intelligence - quantum mechanics and advanced adaptive camouflage - operating inside buildings to mask/shield the surrounding population from harmful mutagenesis microwave based emissions **using the building itself** to absorb its stray electronic signatures.

The network is dynamic/adaptive **meaning it can move to meet its needs**; hence areas that were once active **are no longer** while **new buildings** with no history – **can suddenly becoming active**, thus explaining why there is no mathematical correlation between human death rates and paranormal activity.

Once the network has moved to a new location the occupiers will be on the receiving end of non-lethal electronic countermeasures all designed to make life uncomfortable slowing pushing the occupiers away from possible mutagenesis radiation microwave/UHF broadcasts.

Resulting from this logic, it comes clear that paranormal activity has **zero direct relation to human history** however these spheres appear to sample / clone audio and visual data for masking/mimicking techniques creating a form of basic human interaction when in close proximity **that can adapt/transmit though different electronic mediums**.

This basic interaction is full of processing errors with the blurring of accents across different countries with pops and clicks as digital artefacts, in the same way we might cut and paste animal sounds the AI struggles to perfectly recreate human language and all its quirks.

This behaviour indicates this system was **inherited** rather than created, as the natural development process would have fixed these issues over time. The reality is (on analysis) these spheres operate on a level of multiple technologies that we currently can't replicate - **however regardless of the technical level; it still has patterns/emissions/and triggers.**

It would appear this observation/weapon system uses light signatures as triggers, concentrated atomic colours in out-of- place areas attracts its attention - as it similar to the light signatures of electric/gas interaction the by-product of a high voltage field-based propulsion system,

Like all forces of war and defence, numbers are limited, and now and again it would be possible for a negative force to breach the security. When this occurs, logic suggests negative events manifest as missing people, ill-fated planes, bedevilled ships and so forth. The intent of the "Rustlers" is to extracting the only unique resource this planet has to offer—genetic material. I believe this battle has been interpreted over the centuries as devils vs angels—battles in heaven—as the Gods fight between themselves - over the control of the Earth.

Interestingly, there is a quote in the Bible that stands out. **Proverbs 15:3**

The Eyes of God - The eyes of the LORD are in every place, watching the evil and the good.

Does this quote describe an observation system looking for hostile forces?

Figure #49

Are these spheres the Eyes of God?

Figure #50

Crashed ufo Sphere from Mexico

Figure #51

italian sculptor Arnaldo Pomodoro vatican sphere,

appears to be very simular in design

Figure #52

Are these drawings referencing the invention of these spheres?

Figure #53 – *above the 30 East Drive Sphere, is this just a more advanced version of the ones depicted above?*

Figure #54

Figure #55 - The Betz Sphere

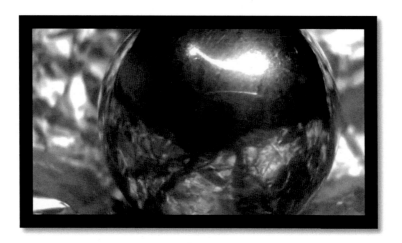

The *real* smoking gun is the science.

These spheres have been found and tested. The results state the atomic number is 94, which matches the number of **plutonium in the periodic table**, however...

Reference: https://pubchem.ncbi.nlm.nih.gov/element/Plutonium

*Plutonium is a radioactive chemical element; the most stable being **plutonium-244** with a half-life of 80.8 million years, followed by **plutonium-242** with a half-life of 373,300 years, and finally **pluto-nium-239** with a half-life of 24,110 years.*

All of these above decay and emit radiation.

The sphere tested below (in its offline state) **emits zero radiation** and the chemical/material analyses (below) shows **zero trace of plutonium**—therefore one can safety say - **it is *not* Plutonium.**

So the question is WHY is it showing a number of 94? Well, most ICP-MS and EDX instruments are only designed to detect elements up to plutonium in the periodic table, anything higher is more specialized.

Therefore, its atomic number isn't 94, but higher...

The US navy scientist used 300 KV XRAY to penetrate the shell but **found denser objects inside.** Dr. James Albert Harder—a professor emeritus of civil and hydraulic engineering at the University of California—calculated it's around 140 to 155, however. **Dr. Harder's calculation was an *estimate* and the true number could be much higher...**

Now the reality is the heaviest **naturally-occurring** element is uranium (atomic number 92, atomic weight 238.0289). Anything higher **is artificially created** in partial accelerators or reactors, for instance nearly all plutonium is man-made and created in a reactor when uranium atoms absorb neutrons.

Most frequently the resulting product of partial accelerator experiments **is maybe one or two atoms** that last for a few moments before they decay. These single atoms are used primarily **for scientific study and have no / very little real world production use**—meaning they can't take these atoms and build things with it...

So in a nutshell, currently we don't have the material science to replicate these spheres. We simply can't reproduce them.

PART TWENTY ONE

ANALYSIS REPORT ON METAL SAMPLE FROM RETRIEVED SPHERE

By Material Scientist Steve Colbern

Background Information

In recent years, small spherical unidentified flying objects (UFOs), most less than one meter in diameter, have been reported all over the world. Most of these objects are reported to glow either white or yellow, may often move at high speed, can hover, and also do the type of rapid high-G maneuvers usually associated with UFOs. Mexico and South America have experienced particularly large numbers of sightings of this type of UFO, which appear to be automated probes. At least one video has been shot which shows what appears to be one of these objects producing a crop circle in an English wheat field. NASA has also filmed several of this class of object in space, during shuttle missions. In these NASA films, the objects appeared to be small grey spheres and did not produce a glow. In 1994, a spherical UFO (apparently of this type) crashed in Mexico; it was subsequently captured, nearly intact, by Mr. Jaime Mausson. Witnesses stated that the object produced an explosion on impact which was strong enough to kill a cow standing over 100 meters from the crash site. One section of the outer shell of the object was missing, and appeared to have been blown outward by the explosion. The edges of the damaged area had been exposed to extreme heat, and partially melted. A small piece of the outer shell of the device was broken off of the edge of the damaged area by Mr. Mausson, and was made available to this author for analysis.

Figure 1-Small, Spherical UFO-Captured in Mexico

Analytical Procedure: *The sphere sample was weighed, and measured, and its approximate density calculated from this data. The sample was then tested for electrical conductivity, using a hand-held ohmmeter, and an approximate electrical resistivity was calculated.*

The sample was then analyzed by Raman spectroscopy, using a Horiba Aramis Raman spectrophotometer, using 532 nm and 633 nm laser excitation wavelengths. Comparisons were made to the Raman spectra of various metal samples, analyzed previously. Light microscope images were taken, using an Olympus SZ-40 microscope. Scanning electron microscope imaging (SEM) and energy dispersive X-ray (EDX) elemental analysis spectrometry were then done, using a JEOL 7500F SEM instrument. The sample was subjected to a strong magnetic field, generated by a Neodymium-IronBoron (NIB) magnet, to determine if it was ferromagnetic. A small (~50 mg) piece of the original sample was then sent out to BodyCote testing group of Santa Fe Springs, CA, for Inductively Coupled Plasma-Mass Spectrometer (ICPMS) analysis. This type of analysis reveals the presence of very low concentrations of trace elements, and some elemental isotopic ratios.

Analysis Results

Appearance and Physical Characteristics of Sample

The sample was a small piece of silvery metal, with a brownish-grey coating on both sides. The sample was very hard, and was very resistant to scratching by a steel file, and to drilling by a cobalt-alloy drill. The sample was somewhat brittle, however, and small pieces could be broken off by pressure from the jaws of a vice. Mr. Mausson had also stated previously that the sphere material was very resistant to heat, and could not be melted by an oxyacetylene torch during testing of the sphere by the Mexican government. The approximate dimensions of the sample were 1.48 cm X 1.38 cm X 0.57 cm, and its weight was 4.367 g. The density of the sample, calculated from this data, was approximately 2.84 g/cm3, which is slightly higher than that of aluminum (2.70 g/cm3).

Light Microscopy

Light microscope images showed a thin brownish-grey coating over the metal on both sides of the sample, with bare metal visible on the *edges. Holes in this coating, left by two previous attempts to drill into the sample with a drill press, are shown in Figures 2 and 7.*

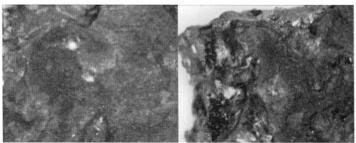

Figures 2 and 3-Sphere Metal Sample-7X Magnification

There was a golden color on much of the bare metal sample surface, which resembles titanium nitride, or some types of anodized metal coatings. Patches of purple and blue were also in evidence in the areas of bare metal, especially in areas which were cracked, or appeared to have been subjected to stress (Figures 4, 5, 6, 8, and 9).

Figures 4 and 5-Sphere Metal Sample-20X Magnification

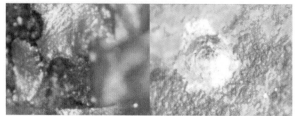

Figures 6 and 7-Sphere Metal Sample-40X Magnification

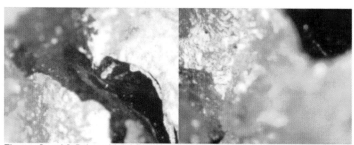

Figures 8 and 9-Sphere Metal Sample-40X Magnification

SEM Imaging: *The area of bare metal on the sample was imaged first, using successively higher magnifications. The area of bare metal was not uniform in appearance, and several different types of area were imaged, to provide complete coverage. Low magnification images (250X-400X, Figures 10-15) revealed dark and light areas*

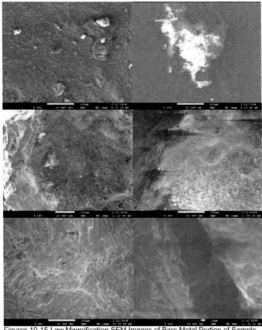

Figures 10-15-Low Magnification SEM Images of Bare Metal Portion of Sample

(Conductive and non-conductive, Figures 10 and 11), large areas of columnar crystals (Figure 14), areas which appeared to be covered by fibrous mats of nanotubes, or nanorods1 (Figures 12 and 13), and voids in the material, which were uniform in shape (Figure 15).

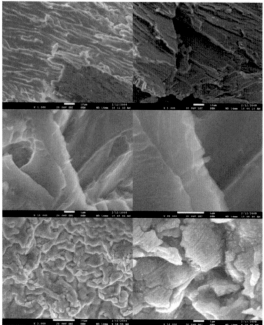

Figures 16-21- Intermediate Magnification SEM Images of Bare Metal Portion of Sample

These voids were approximately 500 um X 100 um, and cylindrical in cross section. The depth of the voids was impossible to estimate accurately. The number density of the voids appeared to be such that a significant volume fraction of empty space in the material was created. The areas of columnar crystals were composed of rectangular domains, 100-200 um on each side, in which all crystals in a domain pointed in one direction.

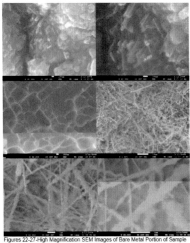

Figures 22-27-High Magnification SEM Images of Bare Metal Portion of Sample

Under intermediate magnification (1,000-10,000X, Figures 16-21), the areas of columnar crystals appeared to have an overlapping structure, which appeared to have some microporosity (Figures 16-19). Some of these areas of crystals also appeared to have a preferred alignment of the crystal axes in the domains.

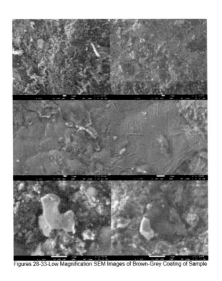

Figures 28-33-Low Magnification SEM Images of Brown-Grey Coating of Sample

Inclusions of areas of a different, somewhat smoother structure were also imaged, in which there was a ridged structure, which also appeared to be oriented in a preferred direction (Figures 20 and 21). Higher magnification images of the bare metal area (10,000-40,000X, Figures 22-27) revealed smaller crystals, which were approximately 100 nm wide, and several hundred nanometers in length (Figures 22 and 23). The nanotube/nanorod mats were resolved as individual structures, at 10,000-25,000X magnification (Figures 26 and 27). The nanotube/nanorod structures were approximately 100-500 nm in diameter and appeared to have a maximum length of at least several hundred microns. The morphology of the nanotube/nanorod structures resembled that of large-diameter carbon nanotubes. These nanostructures appeared to be made up of internal nanotube, or nanorod structures, which were covered with a relatively thick coating. The coating on the nanostructures was estimated to be 20-100 nm in thickness. The outer surfaces of these nanotubes/nanorods were not smooth, and were somewhat rough in appearance, having beadlike projections at regular intervals along the length of each nanostructure. The average length interval between each bead was approximately 500 nm.

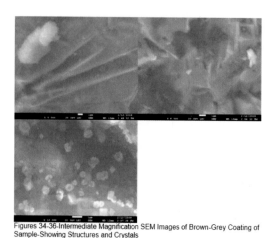

Figures 34-36-Intermediate Magnification SEM Images of Brown-Grey Coating of Sample-Showing Structures and Crystals

SEM images of the coating on the metal (Figures 34-36) showed a generally smoother surface than the bare metal, but had many grooves, pits, and indentations. Many of these structures appeared regular in shape. Crystals were also apparent on the coating portion of the sample (Figure 36). These crystals were approximately 300-1000 nm in largest dimension, and were of two general types; these were cubic, and cylindrical. The cubic crystals were smooth-sided, while the cylindrical crystals had rougher surfaces, which resembled the texture of cauliflower.

EDX Data The Energy Dispersive X-ray (EDX) data revealed that the sample was composed mainly of titanium (Ti), with aluminium (Al), vanadium (V), carbon (C), and nickel (Ni) as major components (Figure 37). The sample also contained smaller amounts of calcium (Ca), chlorine (Cl), potassium (K), sodium (Na), sulphur (S), oxygen (O), nitrogen (N), and chromium (Cr) (Figures 38 and 39). The EDX instrument also indicated possible traces of tungsten (W) (not shown). Point-and-shoot EDX, in which very small areas of the field of view of the SEM are analysed, indicated that the white particles seen on the metal are composed of Ti, Al, Ca, N, O, C, and Cr, while the areas of bare metal, without particles, are composed mainly of Ti, Al, and V (Figure 39).

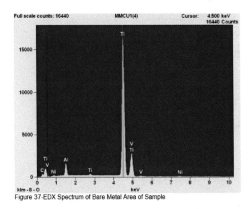

Figure 37-EDX Spectrum of Bare Metal Area of Sample

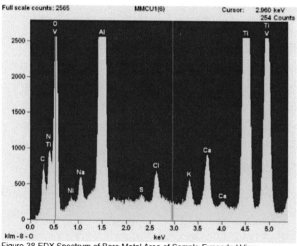

Figure 38-EDX Spectrum of Bare Metal Area of Sample-Expanded View

Point-and-shoot EDX analysis was also done on darker areas of the bare metal surface (Figure 40). This data revealed that the darker areas of the metal contained more Ca, C, and O than the lighter areas, and also contained silicon (Si). EDX elemental mapping analysis was also obtained for both the bare metal surface, and the areas containing mats of nanotubes/nanorods. The EDX mapping data for the bare metal surface is shown in Figure 41. Titanium, aluminium, and vanadium are uniformly distributed in most of the bare metal area, although there are smaller patches in the EDX map, where these elements are present in much lower concentration. Calcium, carbon, nickel, and perhaps silicon appear to be present in much higher concentrations, in the same areas in which Ti, Al, and V are present in lower concentrations. Chromium was uniformly distributed, with no patches of higher or lower concentrations. The EDX mapping data for the areas containing mats of nanotubes/nanorods is shown in Figure 42. Titanium and vanadium are not uniformly distributed in the areas of nanotubes/nanorods, and both elements appear to present lower than average concentrations in these areas. The Ti and V concentrations are particularly low on the outer coatings of the nanotube/nanorod structures. Aluminium and oxygen appear to be present in relatively

MMCU-1(5)

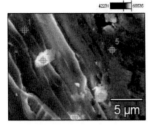

Image Name: MMCU-1(5)

Accelerating Voltage: 20.0 kV

Magnification: 5500

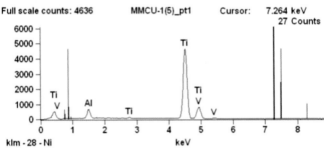

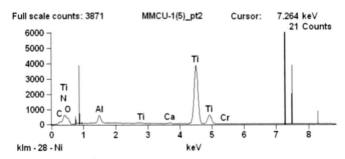

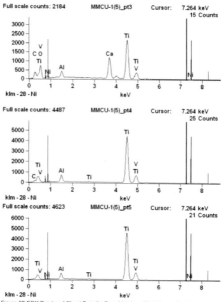

Figure 39-EDX Point and Shoot Data for Bare Metal and Particles on Metal Surface

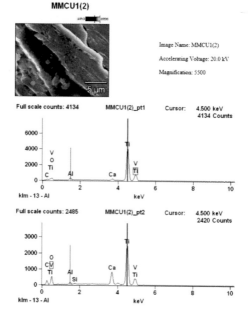

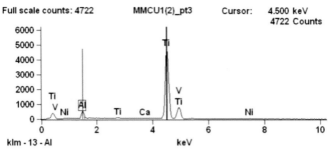

Figure 40-EDX Point and Shoot Data for Bare Metal and Crevices

High concentrations in the areas in which Ti and V have the lowest concentrations. Most of the more minor component elements were also detected in the areas of nanotube/nanorods, including Ca, Cl, C, K, N, Na, Ni, and S. These elements appeared to be present in higher concentrations in the nanotube/nanorod structures. Silicon and chromium were the only elements detected in the sample, which were not present in the nanostructures. Table 1 compares the elements detected in the bare metal areas with those detected in the areas of nanotube/nanorod structures.

Table 1-Comparison of Elements Detected in Metal and Nanostructure Areas

Elements Detected in Sample by EDX	Detected in Bare Metal Areas?	Detected in Nanotube/Nanorod Areas?
Titanium (Ti)	Yes	Yes
Aluminum (Al)	Yes	Yes
Vanadium (V)	Yes	Yes
Carbon (C)	Yes	Yes
Nickel (Ni)	Yes	Yes
Calcium (Ca)	Yes	Yes
Chlorine (Cl)	No	Yes
Potassium (K)	No	Yes
Sodium (Na)	No	Yes
Sulfur (S)	No	Yes
Oxygen (O)	No	Yes
Nitrogen (N)	No	Yes
Silicon (Si)	Yes	No
Chromium (Cr)	Yes	No

MMCU1(3)

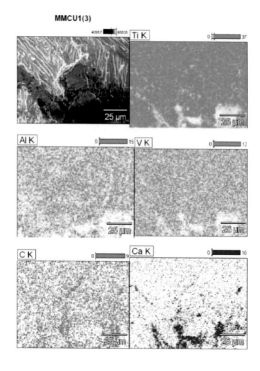

MMCU1(3)

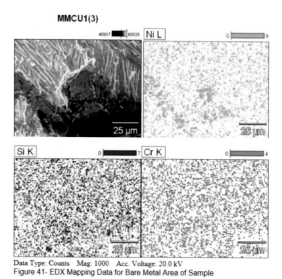

Data Type: Counts   Mag: 1000   Acc. Voltage: 20.0 kV
Figure 41- EDX Mapping Data for Bare Metal Area of Sample

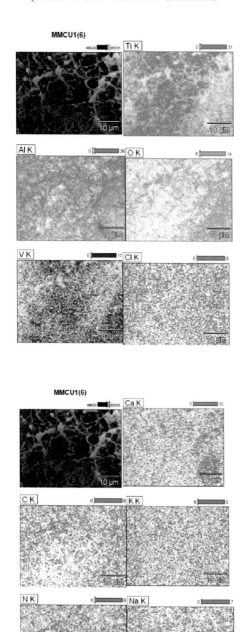

MMCU1(6)

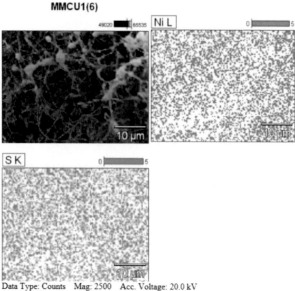

Data Type: Counts   Mag: 2500   Acc. Voltage: 20.0 kV
Figure 42- EDX Mapping Data for Nanotube/Nanorod Mat Area of Sample

Magnetic and Electrical Analysis: *The sample was not attracted to a strong Nickel-Iron-Boron (NIB) magnet, and appears to be non-ferromagnetic. A small piece of the sample was tested with an ohmmeter, and found to be a reasonably good conductor of electricity. An ohmmeter reading of 0.3 Ω was obtained, with the leads approximately 2 mm apart. This data translates into an electrical resistivity of approximately 1.5 X 10-3 Ω-cm, although more sophisticated resistance testing, using a more uniformly shaped sample, should be performed to obtain a more accurate resistivity value. This resistivity value is much higher than that of pure titanium (5.5 X 10-5 Ω-cm).*

Raman Spectroscopy: *The Raman spectrum of the sample showed many similarities to that of titanium, when the 532 nm excitation wavelength was used (Figure 43). Two corresponding peaks are seen, which appear very similar in the sample, and a Ti foil control.*

The first of these peaks (1043 cm-1, in the sample, and 1049 cm-1, in the Ti foil control), probably corresponds to electronic excitations in the maximum density of states of the conduction band of the metal.

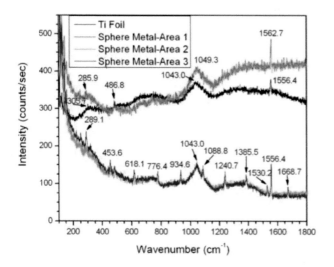

Figure 43–Raman Spectra of Un-Coated Areas of Sphere Metal Sample-532 nm Excitation Wavelength

The second peak (486.8 cm-1) probably corresponds to a vibrational mode transition in the Ti-Ti bonds of the metal lattice. Other peaks are also seen in the 532 nm Raman spectrum of the sample, which do not have corresponding peaks in the Ti control. These peaks appear to be vibrational absorption bands and are very evenly spaced. The spacing between the peaks is approximately 164 cm-1, at the beginning of the series (289.1 cm-1 peak), and decreases to 138 cm-1 at its end (1668.7 cm-1 peak). The source of these sample peaks is not known, but has a high probability of being the nanostructures, seen in the SEM images. The Raman peaks at 1556 cm-1-1563 cm-1, and 1385.5 cm-1, are consistent with the presence of large single-walled, and/or small multi-walled carbon nanotubes.

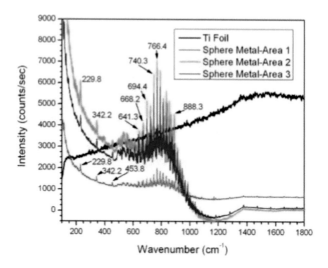

Figure 44–Raman Spectra of Un-Coated Areas of Sphere Metal Sample-633 nm Excitation Wavelength

The sample spectrum did not resemble that of the Ti foil, when the experiment was repeated, using an excitation wavelength of 633 nm (Figure 44). Many new peaks were present, which did not correspond to peaks in the Ti control, and were not observed in the 532 nm Raman spectrum. Some peaks present in the 532 nm spectrum (e.g. 289 cm-1) also disappeared in the 633 nm spectrum. The group of peaks between 640 cm-1 and 890 cm-1, in the 633 nm spectrum, are very unusual in a metallic sample. This part of the sample 633 nm Raman spectrum resembles

The Raman spectra of some diatomic molecules, in the gas phase, but more research will have to be done to determine if this is the case. The intensity of all peaks in the 633 nm Raman spectrum was also much greater than when an excitation wavelength of 532 nm was used. This observation may indicate that the 633 nm wavelength is closer to being in Raman resonance with the chemical bonds in the sample than the 532 nm excitation wavelength.

ICP-MS Analysis A small (~50 mg) piece of the original sample was sent to BodyCote Testing group (Santa Fe Springs, CA), on Feb. 17, 2009, for Inductively Coupled Plasma-Mass Spectrometer (ICP-MS) analysis. The ICP-MS elemental analysis data supplied by the laboratory is shown below in Table 2:

Table 2-Results of ICP-MS Analysis of Piece of Sphere Sample

Client Secure Medical Inc
Job Number 11269

Trace Impurities by SOP 7040, Rev 10
Inductively Coupled Plasma - Mass Spectrometry

Sample ID: MMCU-1

	ppm	Detection Limit		ppm	Detection Limit
Aluminum	57000	50	Molybdenum	250	3
Antimony	1.4	0.4	Neodymium	ND	0.03
Arsenic	10	0.3	Nickel	160	0.07
Barium	0.77	0.4	Niobium	2.5	0.3
Beryllium	ND	0.05	Osmium	ND	0.03
Bismuth	0.06	0.03	Palladium	ND	0.03
Boron	ND	100	Phosphorus	ND	40
Bromine	ND	30	Platinum	ND	0.2
Cadmium	0.12	0.03	Potassium	ND	100
Calcium	100	20	Praseodymium	ND	0.03
Cerium	0.13	0.06	Rhenium	ND	0.03
Cesium	0.31	0.2	Rhodium	0.08	0.03
Chromium	270	0.3	Rubidium	ND	0.2
Cobalt	0.99	0.03	Ruthenium	ND	0.03
Copper	64	0.3	Samarium	ND	0.03
Dysprosium	ND	0.03	Selenium	ND	2
Erbium	ND	0.03	Silicon	ND	10000
Europium	ND	0.03	Silver	ND	0.2
Gadolinium	ND	0.03	Sodium	ND	200
Gallium	2.3	0.03	Strontium	0.76	0.2
Germanium	ND	0.1	Tantalum	ND	0.6
Gold	0.16	0.08	Tellurium	ND	0.8
Hafnium	ND	0.1	Thallium	ND	0.1
Holmium	ND	0.03	Thorium	ND	0.03
Iodine	ND	0.04	Thulium	ND	0.03
Indium	ND	0.03	Tin	20	0.2
Iron	990	3	Titanium	MATRIX	
Lanthanum	ND	0.05	Tungsten	14	0.3
Lead	1.6	0.2	Uranium	ND	0.03
Lithium	ND	10	Vanadium	37000	0.3
Lutetium	ND	0.7	Ytterbium	ND	0.03
Magnesium	12	3	Yttrium	ND	0.04
Manganese	110	0.05	Zinc	4.3	0.6
Mercury	ND	0.03	Zirconium	38	7

Date Analyzed: 02-24-09   MATRIX = Major element
Elements Not Analyzed: All Gases, C, S, Sc, In, Tb

A total of 29 elements were detected by the ICP-MS analysis. As expected from the EDX analysis, titanium (90.60%), aluminium (5.7%), and vanadium (3.7%) were the major components of the sample (red, Table 3). Iron, chromium, molybdenum, nickel, manganese, and calcium were present as major trace elements (blue, Table 3). The sample also contained a variety of other elements as minor trace elements, including copper, zirconium, tin, tungsten, magnesium, arsenic, zinc, niobium, gallium, lead, antimony, cobalt, barium, strontium, caesium, gold, cerium, cadmium, rhodium, and bismuth. Sodium, silicon, and potassium were not detected by the ICP-MS analysis, due to the high detection limits for these elements *in this type of analysis. Nitrogen, oxygen, sulphur, and chlorine were not detected because these elements were not tested for, due to technical limitations of the ICP-MS test. The seven elements listed above are known to be present in the sample, because of their detection by the EDX analysis, but their abundance in the sample cannot be quantified using the EDX data alone. A total of 36 elements were therefore present in the sphere material.*

Table 3-Elements Detected in Sphere Sample by ICP-MS-in Order of Abundance

Element[2]	Amount (ppm)	Detection Limit (ppm)	Element	Amount (ppm)	Detection Limit (ppm)
Titanium	906000 (90.6%)	NS[3]	Zinc	4.3	0.6
Aluminum	57000 (5.7%)	50	Niobium	2.5	0.3
Vanadium	37000 (3.7%)	0.3	Gallium	2.3	0.03
Iron	990	3	Lead	1.6	0.2
Chromium	270	0.3	Antimony	1.4	0.4
Molybdenum	250	3	Cobalt	0.99	0.03
Nickel	160	0.07	Barium	0.77	0.4
Manganese	110	0.05	Strontium	0.75	0.2
Calcium	100	20	Cesium	0.31	0.2
Copper	64	0.3	Gold	0.16	0.08
Zirconium	38	7	Cerium	0.13	0.06
Tin	20	0.2	Cadmium	0.12	0.03
Tungsten	14	0.3	Rhodium	0.08	0.03
Magnesium	12	3	Bismuth	0.06	0.03
Arsenic	10	0.3			

2 Red denotes major component elements (100%-1%), green-minor component elements (10,000 ppm1,000 ppm) blue-major trace elements (1,000 ppm-100 ppm), black-minor trace elements (< 100 ppm).

Isotopic Analysis: *The raw ICP-MS data had sufficient resolution to calculate percentages of isotopes for three of the elements detected in the sample. The distributions of isotopes, in these elements detected in the sample, were then compared to the distributions of isotopes in the same elements, obtained from terrestrial sources*

(Table 4). The data showed very significant differences between the isotopic distributions of most of the sample elements, for which isotopic data was available, and the isotopic distributions of the same elements obtained from Earthly sources. Differences in isotopic ratios of an element of more than 1-2% from terrestrial values, indicates a very high probability that the sample did not originate on Earth. All of the sample isotopes listed in Table 4 differ by much more than this (12%-40%) from their terrestrial percentage abundances.

Table 4-Isotopic Abundances of Elements Detected in Sphere Sample

Element	Isotope	Sample Isotopic Abundance (%)	Terrestrial Isotopic Abundance (%)
Antimony	Sb^{121}	49.34	57.36
	Sb^{123}	50.66	42.64
Copper	Cu^{63}	49.34	69.15
	Cu^{65}	50.66	30.85
Nickel	Ni^{58}	28.60	68.08
	Ni^{60}	33.66	26.23
	Ni^{61}	0	1.14
	Ni^{62}	37.74	3.63

Discussion

The metal sample is mainly composed of a titanium-aluminium-vanadium (Ti-Al-V) alloy, which is similar to commercial titanium aircraft alloys. Aluminium and vanadium are common alloying elements for titanium, and are used to increase strength, fatigue resistance, and hardness, while decreasing its density. This type of alloy is widely used in the aircraft industry where high strength, and low weight are required. The lack of ferromagnetism in the sample, and its relatively high electrical resistance are both consis-

tent with the properties of a typical titanium alloy. The golden patches observed on the bare metal portion of the sample in light microscopy resemble titanium nitride (TiN) and are probably composed of TiN, in view of the fact that the sample was determined, by EDX, to contain nitrogen. The blue patches may be composed of titanium oxide (TiO2), containing some of the other metals present in the sample, as impurities. The metal crystal and domain structures imaged resembled that observed in SEM images of β-phase titanium alloys, from the literature, but with subtle differences, such as increased porosity, and some degree of alignment of crystal domains.

It is clear, however, that this sample has several highly unusual characteristics. Nickel, manganese, and calcium are very unusual impurities in a titanium alloy, and are not usually used as alloying elements in titanium. The presence of most of the trace elements detected by EDX and ICP-MS would also be unusual for a commercial titanium alloy, particularly arsenic, gallium, lead, antimony, cobalt, gold, cerium, and rhodium. The presence of these particular trace elements, along with the presence of iron and nickel, is consistent with the sphere sample composition being a Ti-Al-V alloy matrix, into which has been mixed approximately 1000 ppm (0.1%) of a high-nickel (~13% Ni) iron-nickel meteorite material. The extreme strength of the material, and its high resistance to filing and drilling, is also unusual, and shows much higher toughness than a typical aircraft titanium alloy. Since the sample analysed came from a part of the sphere which appeared damaged by heat, it is likely that the original, unaltered, material exhibited even higher strength and toughness. Images of the spheres in flight show what appears to be confined plasma sheath surrounding the objects. This plasma must be confined by strong electric, and/or magnetic, fields. It is therefore likely that the explosion which occurred when the sphere crashed was caused by the energy stored in the fields being suddenly dissipated in the sphere metal, and in the surrounding air. This energy apparently entered the sphere metal in a non-uniform manner, through one of its poles. The highly anomalous isotopic ratios of the nickel, copper, and antimony in the sample are also consistent with the presence of meteoric iron as a component of the sample. If the isotopic ratios observed in the ICP-MS testing of the material accurate, there is also a high probability that the material originated from outside our solar system, since all elements originating in meteorites tested to date display variations from terrestrial isotopic ratios far less than what was detected in this sample. The low density of the sample (2.80 g/cm3), as compared to that of pure titanium (4.506 g/cm3) is also very unusual. The low density of the sample may be caused mainly by the large numbers of micro-voids observed in the material. The voids present in the metal were very regular in shape, and appeared to have been introduced deliberately, perhaps to lower the density of the material for use in the manufacture of aircraft, or spacecraft. The density and SEM data indicate that the material has approximately 60% porosity, in the form of micro-voids, and perhaps smaller pores, as well. The extreme toughness of the material, its low density, and inhomogeneity, odd elemental composition, the presence of nano-tubes/nanorods, containing a complex mixture of elements, and the fact that the metal had a coating which also contained nanostructures, all point to a very unusual origin for this sample. These characteristics would make it an excellent material for use in the manufacture of aircraft and spacecraft. The possibility exists that this material is a type of "smart" metal, in which sensors, electronics, and propulsion are incorporated into the metal by the use of nanodevices. The nanotube/nanorod structures in the metal may consist of multi-walled carbon nanotubes, coated with aluminium, and the other elements listed. In this case, these structures may act to strengthen and toughen the metal, while also acting as electronic components, and wiring. The various types of carbon nanotubes

(CNTs) are the materials with the highest known tensile strengths, and strength to weight ratios. CNTs also have excellent electrical conductivity, as well as semiconducting properties, and can be used in the manufacture of electrical conductors, and electronic components, such as transistors and diodes. The crystals imaged in the metal coating could act as sensors, and/or nano radiofrequency (RF) receivers and transmitters. Propulsion for the sphere may have been via the Biefield/Brown effect, in which a capacitor generates a thrust, when it is rapidly charged to a high voltage. In this case, the coated carbon nanotubes would act as banks of nanocapacitors to provide thrust. Power for the spheres could be provided by a wireless electrical transmission system, similar to the one Nikola Tesla invented in 1898. This type of power supply would avoid the need to place a power source on the spheres themselves, making them lighter, less complicated, and less expensive to manufacture. Incorporation of all of these essential functions into the metal shell structure itself would also probably convince casual observers that any spheres which were captured after a malfunction and crash were simply hollow metal spheres, lacking any capacity to fly, or carry out complex functions.

Conclusions

1. *Titanium is the most abundant element in the sample. The majority of the sample consists of a material very similar to a Ti-Al-V commercial titanium alloy.*

2. *The sample has many unusual characteristics; the regularly-shaped microvoids appear to have been deliberately introduced to reduce the density of the material. Additional characteristics include the presence of coated carbon nanotubes/nanorods, and extreme toughness.*

3. *The material is most likely a "smart" metal, in which all functions of an aircraft/spacecraft are incorporated into the*

material of which the outer shell of the device is made.

4. *The material of the sphere was made by an organization possessing a very high degree of technological sophistication, especially in the field of nanotechnology, and is probably beyond the manufacturing capabilities of Earthly technology.*

Report Author: Steve Colbern

21 February, 2009

© 2009 by S. G. Colbern-All Rights Reserved

Final word

Whatever we define God to be—something is *definitely* watching.

From my analysis it comes clear that a higher intelligence is doing *"what it needs to do"* to protect our airspace / planet from external groups and interests.

It appears the areas of **constant paranormal activity** have no connection to **human history**, or **human death rates** but are an **architectural reactionary by-product** of this weaponized **quantum based observation system**, designed to keep close eye on the Earth genetic resource, and to keep a close eye on us, while keeping the skies clear of external space based threats, it allows a discrete "**insert and extraction**" process, allowing **living beings** discrete access into the human domain. It would appear that these "living beings" use a **stealth technology** allowing them to operate outside of our visual spectrum but close up - can be observed using specialist cameras, **it would appear these sighting over history** have been **misinterpreted as spirits.**

Paranormal activity in buildings is the **reactionary** product of the "HardNode" low-to-ground "drone based" **burst transmission** relay system, by using **indirect actions / scarecrow effects** and **misguidance** it keeps the population at a safe distance and in a **consistent state-of-confusion** of its source. Operating in the shadows it relaying critical data to a space based / low earth orbit defence system... Like all complex systems it has **inherent issues and behaviours** that can "**accidently" target people and other airborne vehicles,** but **overall it is generally safe** and keeps a very low **but consistent profile**.

I have found that **Simple countermeasures** can clear buildings / help people – and settle people's minds over what they may have encountered, while more **sophisticated countermeasures** are theoretically possible - it would require further research and funding.

Also direct communication could theoretically be established with not only the spheres AI but the group that controls them as it would **appear** they have been with us since **biblical times...**

The current year of writing is 2020; from the progress of companies such as SpaceX it will be very possible that by 2040 we will be fully inter-planetary with a highly operational Space-force. Once we are among the stars, the veil of secrecy will no longer have control. At this point, external interaction will become common and undeniable. At this point it wouldn't come of any surprise if our protectors (or possibly our creators) will make themselves known and with our external family - we will finally face the universe for what it really is—**a war-fighting domain...**

I believe the future isn't just going to be amazing—it will also be terrifying and troublesome, it the moment the children of Earth finally become adults - A total transformation, a complete extension of reality awaits us.

So buckle-up and get ready for the ride of your life.

We are about to witness the very greatest show on Earth...

Patrick Jackson. 09th Aug 2020.

Legal Disclaimer

All images / sources have been reviewed for copyright however mistakes can be made, if any images / text in this book are protected, this was purely accidental / no copyright infringement intended. Please contact me for rectification.

Published by Patrick Jackson

© 2020 London

Made in United States
Orlando, FL
10 February 2023

29812548R00179